PSYCHOLOGY CLASSICS

A Series of Reprints and Translations of Important
Treatises of the Past Dealing with
Psychological Topics

This series is intended to include books and monographs which are needed by psychologists and workers in lines dependent upon or closely related to psychology; and which, because of being out of print or in a foreign language, or both, are not generally enough available. It is hoped that these translations and republications will help to broaden the reading of graduate and undergraduate students, as well as make a wider range of technical material accessible to the layman.

Because of the nature of the work contemplated, it is not expected that the sale of this series will more than repay the cost of manufacture and distribution. Exceptionally favorable arrangements have been made with the publisher, and the labor of editors and translators is without compensation. Specialists in the various fields of psychology are invited to make contributions in the form of transla-ations, and to offer suggestions as to works for which there is especial need of translation or reissue.

Knight Dunlap
Chief Editor

The Johns Hopkins University

A SERIES OF REPRINTS AND TRANSLATIONS

EDITED BY

KNIGHT DUNLAP

THE INFLUENCE OF HABIT
ON THE
FACULTY OF THINKING

BY

MAINE de BIRAN

TRANSLATED BY

MARGARET DONALDSON BOEHM

The Johns Hopkins University

WITH AN INTRODUCTION BY

GEORGE BOAS

GREENWOOD PRESS, PUBLISHERS

WESTPORT, CONNECTICUT

Originally published in 1929 by Williams and Wilkins,
Baltimore

First Greenwood Reprinting in 1970

Library of Congress Card Catalogue Number 79-98854

SBN 8371-3124-3

CONTENTS

VITA

Maine de Biran (1766–1824) was born and lived most of his life in or near Bergerac. His retired life preserved him from the Revolution. It was at this period that he turned to philosophy. After the Reign of Terror he became interested in politics and took part in the commission of 1813, which first gave expression to direct opposition to Napoleon. After the Restoration Biran was treasurer to the chamber of deputies.

INTRODUCTION

Maine de Biran's *Influence of Habit on the Faculty of Thinking*, which is here translated into English for the first time, has become a classic of French psychology. For not only was it the first detailed analysis of habit as a psychological rather than a physiological function, but it became the starting point of French spiritualism which culminated in the philosophy of Henri Bergson.

Biran's essay was written in response to a competition announced by the French Institute, which was to determine "the influence of habit on the faculty of thinking; or, in other words, to show the effect produced by the frequent repetition of the same operations upon our intellectual faculties." But this task had in itself a history which ran back at least to the Abbé de Condillac, who may be considered the founder of French psychology.

Condillac's psychological writings were devoted to an analysis of the content of consciousness into sensations. He posited at the outset of his study a "spiritual substance," the soul, of which the sensations were a "modification." The soul in itself was devoid of character and had no part to play in psychology after it was posited, except that of being "modified." There apparently lingered on in Condillac a remnant of the old Greek theory of causation which was revived to such extraordinary effect in Descartes, Spinoza, and Leibniz, that only similar things could be causally related and that therefore body (or matter) by itself could never "produce" sensations, which were by definition incorporeal entities. Hence one needed a soul which could be their "ground" or "support" or "substance."

But after Condillac. had broken down our ideas into the
sensory elements which gave rise to them, the problem arose
as to how they were combined into new syntheses. It was
clear, for instance that such phenomena as abstract or general
ideas and as the association of ideas in memory, could not be
explained by the soul's activity, for the Condillacist technique
eliminated the possibility of the soul's doing anything. Its
function was to be done unto. Similarly the soul's activity
could not be invoked to explain why a given sensation might
now be remembered, now forgotten, now judged as this or
that, now be seen to be brighter or duller than another. Rousseau and his school, who were anti-sensationalistic, used the
soul whenever an agent of any kind was needed. But Condillac's premises involved explaining all such functions as the
effect of some inherent characteristics of the sensations themselves.

What then were the inherent characteristics of the sensations?

Sensations were first, of course, specific, differing as red from
blue or as a color from a sound. Each was itself. But at the
same time each was not entirely *sui generis;* it was more or less
similar to other sensations. In the third place it had an affective coefficient, being either agreeable or disagreeable. And
finally it had a certain duration, appearing and, after a certain lapse of time, disappearing. Condillac meant by this
that a sensation appears to the subject in consciousness as of
a certain kind, as like or unlike another, as long or brief, as
agreeable or disagreeable. From these traits he hoped to be
able to derive our so-called "mental faculties." Thus specificity would account for "attention," similarity or dissimilarity
for judgment, the affective coefficient for desire and aversion
and in the long run for volition, duration for memory and the
sense of time.

But of these faculties desire alone could arise from a single
sensation. All the others demanded at least two sensations,
for they were all relational in their nature. Even duration

was believed to be ineffectual in itself since all durations would seem instants until their sensations had passed and others had taken their place. But it was reasonable to suppose that a sensation which was agreeable would prove desirable even if it were unique. In the case of the other faculties, then, repetition was necessary, if only to fix their specificity in the mind. And since according to Condillac repetition was the source of habit, habit turned out to be at the root of attention, recall (*ressouvenir*), comparison, judgment, imagination, and recognition. Each of these acts was a habit and became upon repetition easier and easier to perform. When we became accustomed to certain sensations, their similarities were skinned off of them and erected into abstract ideas. When we had frequently experienced two sensations one after the other, the experience of the one would immediately evoke the presence of the other, regardless of the presence of its physical stimulus. Thus habit became of interest not only to the theorist but also to the practitioner. An educator, for instance, would find it very important to know what habits to preserve and what to destroy.

But though Condillac saw the importance of habit, he was not aware of the problems which its presence involved. He saw that the repetition of certain operations would establish them as "second nature," but he seems to have been unaware of the fact that after a certain number of repetitions a habit becomes lost to awareness. If now a comparison was fixed by habit, what would happen when the habit became too usual and thus escaped attention? Should we fail to make the comparison? Again, in the case of general ideas, he failed to ask whether repeated sensations were ever the same or whether the repetition itself did not modify them somewhat. We know how percepts are modified when their stimuli are constantly repeated, how now they grow simpler, now more complex as fatigue or adaptation or interest arises.

These were not the only problems raised and unanswered by Condillac's theory of habit. It was to be expected that his followers would some day put the question of what its nature and effect were. For they had other than theoretical interests in the matter. They were on the whole the representatives of the more constructive Revolutionists who had inherited the liberal and humanitarian program of the Encyclopedists. Their major preoccupation in producing the "new man" which the Encyclopedists had foreseen, was to do away with all supernaturalism in ethics and cognition. If man could be made to stand on his own feet, to seek goodness and truth without ecclesiastical aid, then the Republic would have been, as they saw it, justified. Their opponents, the Rousseauists, were anti-Catholic, it is true, but they were just as fond of supernaturalism as the members of the Church. Their "active" soul—the ancestor of Kant's practical reason—was inscrutable in its ways and beyond the range of psychologists. The followers of Condillac, the *Idéologues* as they were called, had a soul which was subject to scientific investigation and by education capable of just as lofty acts and noble motives. Of this soul habit seemed to be the main spring.

Meanwhile the Swiss biologist and philosopher, Charles Bonnet (1720–1793), had prepared a physiological explanation of habit. In his *Essai de Psychologie* (1754) he suggested that as all sensations depend on nervous currents and as habit is repetition, the repetition of the nervous current makes the resistance to it weaker and thus its passage easier. For when a movement is repeated, he said, the molecular structure of the nerve is somehow changed and this change is naturally fortified by continued repetition. Moreover, this applies not only to nerves but also to organs, limbs, and bodies. As a result physiological habits are established which are the source of our tastes, our inclinations, our manners, our characters. And as the soul seeks pleasure and avoids pains and as it is pleased by that which is facile and avoids the difficult, it seeks those "dispositions" to which it is accustomed and thus the habits which are initiated by our bodies are confirmed by our souls.

Bonnet's theory was as old as Condillac's and as worthy of respect in the eyes of the Idéologues. They asked nothing better than a physiological explanation which was so apparently in accord with dynamics. The ease of passage which was caused by the repetition of nervous currents was like the elimination of friction in the purely physical world. Less and less was there any need for supernatural devices to explain psychological phenomena. The principles of physics and chemistry would suffice. La Mettrie had suggested something like this years before in his *L'Homme Machine* and Cabanis was working out La Mettrie's program in his *Rapports du Physique et du Moral de l'Homme* (1796–1797). Cabanis was, he thought, able to show that our ideas varied with our age, sex, temperament, health, diet and manner of living, and climate. In his writings habit loomed up as capable even of changing temperament which was in those days believed by physicians to be the source of the personal equation, interpreted in the larger sense of the phrase. A sanguine man lived in a sanguine universe, a melancholy man in a universe which was melancholy. Temperament, it was commonly believed, was an innate disposition which colored all our thoughts and from which no one could escape. That habit could alter it, that man could "acquire" a temperament, was an idea which made educators optimistic. Cabanis had an eloquent passage in his book on the effects of habitual surroundings, diet, manner of living. Out of this particular theory, it may be interesting to note in passing, grew a whole *genre* in French literature, the famous "physiologies" of the nineteenth century, first seen in Brillat-Savarin's *Physiologie du Goût*, based upon the physiological notions of Cabanis's pupil, Richerand.[1]

There is perhaps no need to enter into greater details to show why the influence of habit on thought was a living issue in 1800 and thereabouts.

---

[1] At this time habit was utilized in a still more spectacular way by Lamarck to account for the fixation of acquired characters. Habit was for anatomy in Lamarck what it was for psychology in the Idéologues.

Maine de Biran's answer to the question was based upon the principles of Cabanis but, like many another treatise in the history of philosophy, it rose so far above its bases that they were forgotten. Like Destutt de Tracy, the inventor of the word "Ideology" and the chief of the school it signifies, Biran bases all the operations of the mind upon the "faculty of receiving impressions" (i.e., sensory impressions). But all impressions are both active and passive; that is, each is now aroused by a cause external to the individual, now by the individual himself. Passive impressions he calls "sensations," active, "movements," acknowledging his debt to Tracy in utilizing this distinction. But, though Tracy had made the original distinction, what he did not see was that practically each type of impression could be active as well as passive. In Biran there is active touch—"feeling"—as well as passive touch—the "feel" of things; looking as well as seeing; listening as well as hearing; savoring as well as tasting. Only smelling is inactive; "its absolute immobility shows how passive it is;" several odors mixed together blend into one despite the effort of our attention. All we can do to modify it is to inhale slowly. Its very name, "sentir," is properly used as a synonym for "sensing," for it is almost purely sensitive, excelled only by the somatic impressions which are the limit of sensation.

From the differences which there are in the degree of sensitivity (passivity) as contrasted with mobility (activity), Biran hoped to show that the power of perception, or of distinguishing our impressions from one another, did not depend upon our sensitivity, but upon our mobility. But since mobility was for him voluntary effort, it was clear that our power of perception was not a "transformed sensation" in the Condillacist manner, but an effect of something "internal" to the individual.

The rest of the essay is a detailed study of the effects of habit upon our various sensations and movements and upon our "determinations." These latter are the changes which linger on in our minds after the experience of an impression. They are again both passive and active, simple memory and deliberate recall respectively. There is no need of our summarizing his results here, for they are adequately summarized in the Report of Destutt de Tracy appended to this translation. But we may mention—because of its influence—that his conclusion widens the gulf between sensation and perception by pointing out that the former is weakened by habit, the latter strengthened. Hence a purely sensitive being would as his life went on gradually be reduced to a state approaching unconsciousness and would in no wise resemble the statue of Condillac whose mind became, on the contrary, more and more delicately articulated and provided with ideas.

Why was this of any importance to the history of French thought? Because perception—which, it will be remembered, was active—was the result of effort and effort was essentially the same thing as volition. Volition for Condillac was simply a function of sensation; for Biran it was a primitive faculty in itself.

As his thought developed it began to take on more and more importance. First conceived of as simply muscular tension, it began to grow into something which was not only not muscular but not even corporeal. This evolution was aided by Biran's friend, Ampère, the physicist, who was an enthusiastic Kantian. To Ampère what Biran called "effort" or "volition" was purely and simply the Ego, which was supra-sensory and could be known only by a kind of special intuition. This when adopted by Biran led him to interpret the universe subjectivistically, showing how man read the Ego's properties of substantiality, causality, unity, and identity into the external world. But then doubts of a religious nature assailed him and soon he began to feel that the Ego's task in effort was the repression of all evidence of a corporeal world that the "spirit" might be more freely intuited. After that the will became autonomous and supra-rational as in Fichte. Human personality became ineffable and man's one hope lay in mysticism. Effort, as he finally described it, was the effort of the soul to unite itself to God.

These later phases of Biran's thought were not made public for some years—for only his treatises on habit and on the decomposition of thought together with a biographical notice of Leibniz were published in his lifetime. So that he remained for his generation one of the minor Idéologues who had developed some of his master's suggestions. But in 1818 Victor Cousin began his lectures as a professor of philosophy. As a younger man he had attended meetings of Biran's philosophical club and been charmed with the conversations that he had heard. Hence desirous of putting his own philosophy under the banner of a Frenchman, he could find no one more fitting than his former host. Among his pupils was Félix Ravaisson, who was to dominate one wing of French philosophy for many years later. Ravaisson had gone to Germany to study with Cousin's friend, Schelling, and had come back to defend a thesis in the Sorbonne on Biran's original theme of habit. It will be found that he combined Biran's central doctrine of the two kinds of impression, modified so contradictorily by habit, with Schelling's notion of the polarity of all things in the universe, so that the Biranian Will became a sort of Schellingian Absolute.

Ravaisson began by pointing out that habit was found only in living things, never in the inorganic. A stone thrown a hundred times in the air learns nothing, is the same stone at the end as it was at the beginning. Hence habit at the outset is seen to be a modification of something organic which has an "internal" life which may undergo the change. Externally the object need not change, but its internal being becomes modified. But space is the condition of stability, time of change: inorganic beings are essentially spatial, organic temporal. So the changes which occur in the inorganic world are essentially spatial changes, be they locomotion, mechanical balance, electrical interactions, or chemical syntheses. They do not "endure," to use a Bergsonian phrase, they produce no "individuals," they are not subject to habit.

When life enters the scene, its changes produce no new

homogeneous syntheses—such as occur when two chemicals unite—but rather a unity which endures in time through a series of ever changing states. There is thus provided the proper scene for habit to play its rôle upon. Life forms a world of its own, full of "internal" potentialities. A living thing may be said to have its own "nature," which, though conditioned by the laws of matter, is not entirely subject to them. That "nature," which Ravaisson believed was what Aristotle meant by "potency," develops in its own way and is alone what can be modified by habit. Matter and life then are the two poles of his Schellingian universe, the former under the laws of "necessity," essentially spatial, unindividualized, always acted upon from without (receptive), the latter in part self-determined, essentially temporal, highly individualized, acting and growing (spontaneous). By assimilating his concept of matter to Biran's sensitivity, and that of life to Biran's mobility, Ravaisson was able to infer that habit diminished receptivity and increased spontaneity. Similarly as life departs from matter—in the higher stages of evolution—the domain of habit increases. Thus the vegetables are less susceptible to it than the animals, the animals less than man. And in man that part of him which is material must be less susceptible than that which is immaterial—whence the passage by easy stages to an immaterial something, source of our energy and hence of our mobility, initiator of effort, our innermost selves, the Soul.

But for a person trained in German idealism such an apparent conflict in the individual—or elsewhere, for that matter— could not be left "unreconciled." Something must be done to show that receptivity and spontaneity are at heart two "aspects" of the same thing. There must be something which is Spontaneity "at once passive and active, and different both from mechanical Fate and from reflective Liberty."[2] This Spontaneity is exactly what Bergson was to call later the *Élan*

---

[2] De l'Habitude, *Rev. de Metaph. et de Morale*, II (1894), p. 20.

Vital, and Schelling after Plotinus had called the World Soul. The main difference—the only important difference—between Ravaisson and Bergson is that for the former the Vital Force seeks ends and for the latter it is purposeless.

This metaphysical account of habit was the kernel of Ravaisson's system as it developed. Its author expanded it at greater length in his essay on Aristotle's *Metaphysics* and in his report on French philosophy which he made for Napoleon III. We need not follow him on these metaphysical flights; to do so would be beside the point. Let us note merely that the position was more and more solidly entrenched as the years went on and that French spiritualism was largely defended from it until the rise of Bergson. This statement must not be accepted too literally; there were French spiritualists whose immediate forebears were other than Ravaisson. But at the same time the prestige he gave the theory of man as a "free" and spontaneous spirit counted for more than any other one thing in the growth of spiritualism in France.

Bergson's similarity to Ravaisson must be obvious by now to any who have read his works. In him too there appears the Schellingian interplay of receptive and spontaneous beings, the former equated with passivity, matter, space, external change, the latter with activity, life, time, and growth. There are certain substitutions of new words for old, such as "intuition" for "mystic love," but in Ravaisson, as in Schelling and Plotinus, the only way to know the supra-rational is to be it. There is, moreover, in Bergson a greater willingness to acknowledge a sort of anti-intellectualism, though he has always insisted that the intellect alone is capable of knowing matter and space. Yet in Ravaisson one does not find the overt deprecation of "concepts" which appears in his famous successor. Above all, what Bergson adds to the theory is the opinion that habit is essentially the "materializer" as if matter were the habits of the *élan vital*. Thus that which in Ravaisson was an aid to spontaneity as well as to receptivity is in Bergson a hindrance. Intuition has apparently no habits, for it alone can deal with

the novel and the individual.   Habit would seem to be opera-
tive in the realm of intellectual cognition alone.

This is a sketch, then, in miniature of how the theory of
habit developed in nineteenth century France.   It makes no
pretense of being complete, for after all its purpose is simply
to place Maine de Biran's essay in its proper historical setting.
It is but one of the many ironies of history that a work which
was written to make faithful inferences from a given philosophy should serve as the basis of that philosophy's strongest
opponent.   Biran himself in his later years looked upon it
with regret and feared that it might lead the young astray
from the paths of religious and moral rectitude.   That fear
may be set aside as groundless now and the work remains
simply as one of the most brilliant precursors of the analytic
method in introspective psychology.

GEORGE BOAS.

The Johns Hopkins University.

REPORT OF CITIZENS CABANIS, GINGUENÉ, RÉVEILLÈRE-LÉPEAUX, DAUNOU AND DESTUTT-TRACY

Appointed by the Class of Moral and Political Sciences to examine the seven memoirs entered in the competition, upon the question proposed in these terms:

To Determine What is the Influence of Habit upon the Faculty of Thinking; or, in Other Words, to Show the Effect which the Frequent Repetition of the Same Performances Produces upon Each of our Intellectual Faculties.

BY

M. DESTUTT-TRACY

The Institut de France is composed of the five academies, the Académie Française, the Académie des Inscriptions et Belles-Lettres, the Académie de Sciences, the Académie des Beaux-Arts, and the Académie de Sciences Morales et Politiques. It was organized by Daunou during the Revolution and was composed of various "classes", corresponding to the present academies, the second of which is the Académie des Sciences Morales et Politiques. This class was suppressed by Napoleon in 1803. See G. Boas; *French Philosophies of the Romantic Period*, Baltimore, 1925, p. 19.—Tr.

REPORT OF M. DESTUTT-TRACY

The class had proposed this prize subject on the 5th of Vendémiaire, Year VIII. But at the meeting of the 15th of Germinal, Year IX, it was decided that none of the contestants had entirely fulfilled the designs of the Institute; and a new competition was opened on the same subject. It is of this second competition that I was appointed to make a report. The committee of which I am the spokesman has been unanimous on all points.

First, of the seven memoirs which were submitted, it was thought proper to discard five, to wit: numbers 1, 2, 4, 6 and 7. The authors either have not understood the question or have not sufficiently plumbed its depths; and we did not think it necessary to give you a detailed account of them.

Number 5, bearing this motto: *Habit is a second nature*, without being very satisfactory, seemed nevertheless to be more deserving of your attention. It is divided into two parts. The first treats of the knowledge that man imbibes from nature without the help of the communication of ideas; the second treats of the communication of ideas.

The first part is subdivided into two sections: one on the system of self-evident knowledge, the other on the system of knowledge of fact; and this first contains two chapters: one on facts of the physical order, the other on mental facts. This division was not approved. It seemed to presuppose that all the knowledge of which it spoke in the first part could be acquired without the aid of signs, which would be strangely to miscomprehend their influence. The author also seems hardly to regard signs as anything other than means of communicating or at most of classifying our ideas and not to realize sufficiently how necessary they are to form ideas and fix them in our minds.

It appears inadmissible also to put so-called self-evident knowledge in opposition to knowledge of fact. The result is that our different intellectual operations are confused; and that the progress of the human spirit is not traced with enough precision.

Upon the whole, although this memoir is commendable for its ingenious ideas and gives evidence of capacity, it shows that the author has not sufficiently reflected upon his subject, that he has counted too much upon his fluency and that he is not even sufficiently well acquainted with what has been written on these matters. He can only be encouraged to devote himself to this science and then it is likely that he will make progress in it.

Number 3 remains, having for its motto that phrase of Bonnet: *What are all the operations of the soul if not movements and repetitions of movements?* It has already obtained very honorable mention at the meeting of last year. The author has rewritten it; he has profited by the advice which was then given him by the *Institute*, and this time he has won all the votes. As we are all of the opinion that he deserves the prize, I ought, according to your regulations, to limit myself to proposing to you to hear it read, but as it is very voluminous, I am going to try to give you a concise idea of it, although it is very difficult, I should say even impossible, to make a satisfactory analysis of a work of this kind.

Habit is never present to reflection, Mirabeau (*Conseils à un jeune prince*) has said. This maxim has keenly impressed our author, and he has made it the beginning of his work.

He sees in this profound observation the reason why knowledge of our intelligence must be the last of our knowledge to be perfected; why it was very difficult to imagine beginning this study; why in this investigation the spirit of analysis must be continually stopped at each step; in short, why it must have already discovered many things relating to the forms and products of our reasoning, before having discovered the genesis of our ideas, which are its elements; in a word, why the human spirit has always known things better, in proportion as they are further from it and less intimately connected with its existence and with its most frequent acts.

He further finds in this very true reflection, what obliged the creators of the science of ideas (Condillac and Bonnet) to study the human spirit in a hypothetical phantom, the fruit of their imagination. Although necessary in the beginning, this way of proceeding should be followed no longer. It is the works of those early masters and their successors, which to-day enable us to determine the effects of habit, that universal cause of all our progress on the one hand and of all our blindness on the other. But to do it with precision, it is necessary to begin by presenting a concise analysis of our intellectual faculties and of the impressions which we owe to them. This is what the author does immediately after these preliminary observations which already show how thoroughly he is master of his subject. Let us follow him in this investigation.

He prefers to call *impression* what we ordinarily call *sensation*. The reason is that of those sensations some, such as those which come from our internal organs, are solely or almost solely due to the faculty of feeling; others, such as those which the simple movement of our members causes, are solely or almost solely due to the faculty of moving; and finally, almost all are in different degrees composed of the effects of these two faculties combined. But in the same way that physiologists distinguish sensory and motor activities, although they recognize in them a common origin and although together they compose the vital force or the phenomena of life, so he thinks that in ideology, it is necessary to distinguish in the *impression* what belongs to *sensibility* and what belongs to *mobility*, the passive and the active or rather sensory activity and motor activity, the purely affective part and the perceptive part, in a word, *sensation* and *perception*.

He uses these words *perceptive part* and *perception* to designate the portion of the impression which is derived from the faculty of moving, because he thinks that it is to this and to the consciousness of voluntary movement that we owe all our knowledge, even that of our *ego* and that the purely *affective*, purely sensory impressions never enable us to reach any judgment, not even that of *personality*, which consists in perceiving that it is we who exist and feel.

That is what justifies, or at least is the alleged motive for substituting the word *impression* for that of *sensation*. After this distinction of the parts of the impression, he examines, in the exercise of each of our senses, what is the part played by feeling and what by movement.

1. TOUCH

In tactile impressions, it is easy to distinguish passive and active touch, that is to say that which is limited to receiving the impact of objects which approach the organ and that which seeks them by means of a voluntary and felt movement. In this latter kind of touch the effect of *sensory* activity is easily discerned from *motor* activity. It is to mobility that is due the perception of effort, which is composed of the ego which wills to move itself and of the being which opposes it and consists in the judgment that we make of it. That is the first of our judgments, our earliest knowledge and the source of all the rest; it is at the same time the basis of all real existence. The principal organ of touch being the hand, it is of all our senses that in which in general sensibility is the least vivid and mobility greatest. This is why it is touch which teaches us most and teaches all the other senses. When its sensibility is too vivid, it no longer has this prerogative, we have only sensation, perception disappears. It is a general rule that whenever feeling predominates, there is no longer knowledge.

2. SIGHT

The organ of this sense is much more sensitive and less mobile than that of touch. Nevertheless, we may still distinguish passive and active sight, that is to say, the cases where we receive only visual impressions and those where by different movements we direct ourselves towards them and modify the organ in such a manner as to receive them in one way rather than in another.   There is a difference between looking and simply seeing, as between bumping into an object and feeling it (*heurter et tâter*).   Therefore, the action of sensory forces and that of motor forces (feeling and movement) ought to be recognized in the exercise of active sight.   Consequently, the author thinks that active sight alone would produce the impression of effort, would afford opportunity for the knowledge of the *ego* and by that of various other things, would give rise to judgments, in a word, would produce perceptions, although in fewer number than touch would.   But, according to him, the greatest utility of the mobility of the sense of sight, is to be put within reach of associating its operations with that of touch, of which the perceptions are indeed more distinct and persistant because external resistance is there substituted for simple muscular resistances.   "This," he says, "is why every slightly mobile organ, which if it were isolated would transmit only more or less passive and confused impressions, may acquire the activity which it lacks, by its association or its correspondence with an organ superior in mobility."

3. HEARING

The preceding reflection is applied in the happiest manner to the sense of hearing.   The organ of this sense is very sensitive and only slightly mobile; and although there would be, between simply hearing and listening, a difference which is connected with the internal activity of the muscles of the ear, nevertheless hearing ought to be purely passive and sensory. Yet it provides us with a great many very delicate and distinct perceptions.   But this is because it is associated with a highly mobile organ, that of the voice, which repeats and reproduces internally all the sounds by which hearing is affected and thus enables us to distinguish and perceive them.   Moreover we always perceive the sounds and articulations so much the more distinctly the more similarity they have with those which we can imitate and reproduce; and the nicety and delicacy of hearing are always in proportion to the facility and flexibility of the vocal organ. All the observations on different species of animals and on different conditions of man confirm this important reflection. The association of the voice with hearing thus corresponds in its effects with that which exists between touch and sight. That is, in our opinion, a very fine idea and one which gives much weight to the theory of our author.

4. TASTE

The organ of taste is not deprived of mobility. Taste is not completely passive; there is a difference between simply having a sensation of a flavor and tasting it. But taste is highly affective; the impressions that it receives stimulate an important internal organ (the stomach). They powerfully disturb the whole sensory system. Moreover, the resistance which the savory object presents is very transitory; sensation must therefore predominate in taste and perception be almost of no force; also flavors are only slightly distinct and susceptible of recall; also they have few names in languages or names corresponding to touch qualities, as those of odors are taken from visible objects. Only the tastes of solid objects are less confused than those of liquids. They more closely approach perception, which confirms the principle that all knowledge comes from activity.

5. SMELL

Smell is even more passive than taste with which it has much connection. There is again a slight difference between being sensible of an odor and smelling; but the mobility of this sense consists almost entirely in the movement of respiration, a movement continuous, necessary, and consequently profoundly habitual and only slightly voluntary. Moreover, it puts into activity various internal organs and the whole sensory system. Moreover the impressions of smell, as language indicates, are almost wholly in sensation and hardly at all in perception. Then, too, they are affective, confused, impossible to name and to recall, indivisible, imperceptible, uninstructive.

6. THE ORGANIC SENSE

Finally come the impressions which we experience in the internal parts of the body. These are *pure sensations.* Sensory force is alone in activity there. No perceived effort, no distinction, no true memory; all knowledge is eclipsed with the absence of voluntary movement.

Every impression is more or less fitted to be *perceived* or *felt* according as it is more or less closely allied to a voluntary movement and as its affective property is more or less dominant.

Upon this explanation of the functions of our senses are founded further developments.

The effect of impressions upon organs is not simply and solely momentary; they leave durable traces there. But these persisting modifications of the organs the author calls *determinations:* he says that a determination is effected when the organ resumes the same state in which it was by virtue of the first action.

Since there are two sorts of impressions, or rather since the impression includes two different things—*sensation* and *perception*—there must be two sorts of determinations, *sensory* and *perceptive* or *active;* that is to say determinations, which the *sensory* organs contract, must not have the same properties as those which *motor* organs contract.

If the sensory determination be effectuated by the renewed action of the object or spontaneously in its absence, the sensation, the author thinks, will not be recognized to be the same as the first, in other words, there will not take place what he calls *memory*.

On the contrary, let the active determination be effectuated with regard to the same object, the individual is conscious of a renewed and easier effort; he recognizes himself as the willing subject and consequently he recognizes the previously experienced impression. If this happens spontaneously and in the absence of the first cause, the individual, not experiencing the same resistance, must distinguish that it is a memory and not the first impression.

This memory is only a copy of the first perception. The author calls it an *idea:* there is no difference between the idea and the original impression except the sensory part which is not renewed.

Thus without the active determination there would be neither *remembrance* nor *ideas.*

Furthermore there would be neither *signs* nor *memory,* for, according to our author, it is voluntary movements which are the natural—afterwards artificial—signs of impressions; and memory is the faculty of recalling by moving or making an effort.

He calls *imagination* the faculty of involuntarily reproducing certain impressions. He calls these reproductions not ideas but *images.* These images are taken for realities because the consciousness of their active part has disappeared through habit, and because we are struck only by their sensory part. He believes that this applies more often to visual impressions than to others, and that these images are the most immediate products of the activity proper to the cerebral center: hence visions.

It must be admitted that this last part of the introduction does not present the same degree of lucidity as that which contains the analysis of the senses. Perhaps this is because it would have been necessary to make a distinct analysis of our intellectual faculties and perhaps it would have been still better not to subsume pure sensation with *perception* under the single name of *impression.* For this perceptive part of the imagination consists of judgments reached, which joined to the affective part of simple sensation, makes it become a compound idea. But in speaking of this simple sensation and showing successively all the degrees of composition and complexity through which it passes, the explanation of the subsequent intellectual operations might perhaps have been clearer.

Moreover, the sequel will throw light on this obscure point. We must follow our author in the two sections of his work, one which treats of passive habits and the other of active habits. They are full of shrewd bits of insight and curious details.

Passive habits

A universal and well-known fact is that all our impressions whatever they be when they are continued or frequently repeated, grow gradually weaker unless the organ be injured or destroyed. But in growing fainter, some are gradually more and more obscured, others often become more distinct.

When I frequently experience the same degree of temperature or the same odor, I am less affected by it; when I experience it for a long time continuously, I end by feeling nothing.

Other impressions, such as those of sight and hearing grow weaker also through being repeated or continued, but they become more distinct: this is because they include sensation and perception and while sensation is obliterated, perception grows clearer.

The first chapter which treats of continued and repeated sensations is intended to explain the first of these two effects. The author gives an account of sensory activity as follows.

Vital movement, he says, incessantly sustains in all parts of the living being, a certain degree of sensibility proper to each and all of its parts. When this general *tone* is not lowered, the living being may and must have a dull feeling of his existence, but he has no sensation in the strict sense of the term. When he receives an increase or a general diminution, or a sudden weakening in some parts, there is a sensation, but in this last case the irritated organ reacts upon the others, the equilibrium is gradually re-established, and at the most the general tone remains augmented or diminished, sometimes even it is, moreover, one or the other when through the cessation of the irritating cause, the organ which has suffered has already resumed its previous condition; which produces a new inequality in the opposite direction.

This manner of considering the sensory principle, of which I can give here only a glimpse, explains sufficiently well why the same affective cause does not always produce the same effect upon us; why we do not perceive slow and gradual changes which operate in us; why continued sensation degenerates or disappears; why, although less felt, it often becomes more necessary to the sentient being, etc., etc. In a word, it renders a satisfactory account of the divers phenomena of sensation in the strict sense of the term. But the perceptive part of our impressions does not follow the same laws; it is the subject of the following chapter.

While repeated sensation only succeeds in being obscured and extinguished, all that pertains to the activity of our motor organs is perfected by exercise and all the operations of our active senses become easier, quicker, more distinct in proportion as they are more frequently repeated; it is these which produce perception; it is to it that we owe all our progress and our errors. The author assigns three causes of their improvement: 1st, the diminution of the sensory effect; 2nd, the increasing facility of movements; 3rd, their association in the cerebral center with other movements or other impressions which serve as *signs* for them. We shall not follow him in the development of the effects of these causes; one should read in the work itself the statement of the facts which manifest the action, of each of them; but, in the third chapter, the associated perceptions and the diverse judgments of habit which result from them are especially examined.

Bacon remarked, with very great sagacity, that human intelligence is like an uneven mirror which mingles its own nature with that of the objects which it reflects. And our author adds that the nature of the understanding is nothing else but the totality of habits characteristic of the cerebral organ, which he regards as the universal sense of *perception*, whereas sensations are the effects of particular senses and external organs. Determinations, habits contracted by this central organ and persisting in it, constitute what he calls our imagination; and it is this faculty which, reacting upon the products of the external senses, becomes the "uneven mirror" of Bacon. It is this which, on the occasion of one of the perceptions which it has associated together, reproduces instantly all the others in such a way that they serve each other reciprocally as signs in consequence of the habitual connections which they have previously had.   Hence the multitude and the rapidity of our judgments, but also their boldness; hence it happens that the child calls every man *papa* and that man attributes a will like his own to everything that acts.   The author considers the effects of the imagination in the perceptions which it has associated through simultaneity or succession.   He notes its different consequences, and he concludes that, in the present state of our faculties, every perception is composed of a host of habitual judgments which become rapid, easy, and by that very fact apparently unimportant to the point of slipping out of the consciousness of the individual in whose brain they occur The greatest proof that could be given of the existence of this multitude of judgments of which we are often unaware, which brings it about that the impression which seems to us the simplest is really a very complicated perception, is the feeling of surprise which we experience every time that their ordinary connection is deranged in a phenomenon which is outside the common order.

The author takes occasion to explain particularly, in Chapter IV, the effects of habit on the moral feelings which result from these perceptions, which feelings he regards as sensations proper to the cerebral organ and the imagination.   He discovers especially the causes of superstitious ideas and instinctive determinations.   This chapter is full of very fine observations.

Here ends the first section, entitled: *Passive habits.*   In order not to feel that it contains things foreign to what this title promises, it is necessary to recall that if not only sensa-

tion or the passive part of the impression is treated there, but
even perception, which is the active part of it, it is because it
enters into the composition of the products of the imagination,
which the author regards as the sensibility characteristic of the
cerebral organ.   There is perhaps something hypothetical
about that which is not sufficiently justified by physiological
observations and which one could have done without, as I have
already shown, by considering the formation of perception
from another point of view.   But this manner of considering
phenomena leads to such interesting and instructive developments, that we cannot regret it.   Let us then continue our
account of the work and of the second section, which treats of
active habits.

SECOND SECTION

*Active habits or the repetition of operations which are founded upon
the use of voluntary and articulated signs*

This second part is almost entirely the record of the articulated signs and of the different effects which their repeated use
produces upon our divers sorts of impressions.   The author
begins by recognizing two kinds of natural signs; every impression, even purely sensory, which is associated through
habit with other impressions, becomes their sign, and reciprocally, that is to say, that it awakes them and is awakened by
them.   But these kinds of signs are not free, i.e., do not depend upon the will of the individual; it is these that affect us.
We imagine without knowing, without perceiving, without
being able to be certain of the reality of the impression which
we experience.   They leave no room for the activity of reflection; their effect is mechanical and forced.   These are, according to the author, the signs of the *imagination;* this is why he
calls the imagination a passive faculty, like *sensibility.*

Another sort of natural signs is the voluntary movements
associated naturally with our impressions which constitute
their perceptive part.   These produce knowledge, perception,
judgment because they are accompanied by the impression of

effort which is the product of the feeling of the *ego*, of that of resistance and of a judgment.   These depend upon the individual; they are at his command, they furnish a basis for voluntary recall, they are the root of memory in the strict sense of the term.

But the effect of habit is to make the consciousness of the impression of effort gradually disappear, and making the voluntary signs of memory gradually easier, to bring them gradually nearer the state of the passive signs of the imagination. When the motor faculty has come to that degree of perfection on the one hand and of blindness in its exercise on the other, the individual remains passively delivered over to the impulsion of external causes, organic tendencies, involuntary starts and periodic returns of sensibility; he lives in a kind of somnambulism; he has no longer the power to react upon what moves him; he has no longer the capacity for reflection; he has fallen under the absolute sway of his imagination.

The conversion of certain voluntary movements, of certain natural signs of memory, into artificial signs, gives new life to the perceptive ability; it gives a new energy to memory. Voluntary movements of the vocal organ above all have great advantages in producing this effect, but soon habit returns to deform these new signs and to make them approach a state of automatism.   Moreover, they cannot have an equal influence upon the impressions of diverse kinds to which they are united. They cannot revive sensations and perceptions equally; memory is not always completely representative.   Hence the source, according to our author, of three sorts of memory, the mechanical, the sensory and the representative, the effects of which he successively examines.

Articulated sounds or tones abstracted from their representative value, are only simple products of motor activity. Nevertheless, in relation to memory they have a great advantage over other purely muscular movements.   This is because they not only are manifest to consciousness like purely muscular movements by the impression of the *effort* necessary to produce it, but they are further sensible to the individual through the perception that hearing receives of them. Gestures have a similar advantage in that they strike the sight. That is why, in order to remember a series of gestures, it is useful to see them while making them; to remember words, it is well to hear them while articulating them and pronouncing them aloud. Nevertheless, to remember words is only to remember a series of movements, is only a mechanical memory. It becomes representative only when one remembers at the same time perceptions to which these words are attached. Only then is it useful. The awkward manner in which children's mechanical memory is trained, making them learn by heart many words which they understand little if at all, is thus quite capable of increasing this memory, for all movements become easier through exercise, but it is not fitted to make it representative. The trouble which we have to pronounce the words of a very harsh language, the too lively pleasure caused by too harmonious sounds, the arbitrary choice of words destitute of similarity, are so many circumstances which by too exclusively drawing the attention to the sign and by diverting it from perception, contribute to hinder memory from becoming truly representative. Be that as it may, that is what our author calls mechanical memory.

He calls it sensory when the sign serves to reveal the image of those feelings, of those affections of sensibility which he said in the first part are not susceptible of being reproduced in reality, or when it becomes the means of recalling those vague and confused ideas which have never been accompanied by real perception or from which it has disappeared. In these two cases the sign is indeed less a true sign than a means of tumultuous and almost fortuitous excitation, which easily becomes fantastic. Memory of this sort hardly differs from what he calls the imagination. The vicious use of words, the excessive use of metaphors, allusions, tropes, figures of every kind, is suited to give rise to it. Those with whom it prevails are all for passion and strangers to reflection; it produces weakness of will and incapacity of judgment. The author has compared mechanical memory to the physical constitution in which muscular power predominates. He compares sensory memory to that in which sensory power is too excited. It is from the equilibrium and the exact combination of these two forces that a good temperament and a truly representative memory are formed. It remains for us to speak of this.

The idea is the copy of the perception, and, according to our author, we have no real perceptions except those of forms, figures, and sounds and their derivatives, because these are the only impressions which are connected with the activity of the motor force and our active senses. Our other impressions are only sensations, are passive, and because of that very fact are not susceptible of being reproduced at will, *par levibus ventis volucrique simillima somno.* Thus true memory is limited to the *representation* of forms and figures by means of the *recall* of sounds. In fact, representative memory is that in which the sign and the idea are well united and always reproduced together, that is, that in which the sign gives rise to the whole idea. But in order that this be possible, it is necessary that the compound idea be formed entirely of parts susceptible of being reproduced. But, in this case, there is only its perceptive part. Its effective part, the feeling which it produces is not there. It may be more or less excited by the sign, but always tumultuously and irregularly. All of this is due to variable circumstances. But it cannot be truly represented. And this is, nevertheless, the only truly useful effect of the sign for our improvement. Such are the bases upon which are founded the reflections of the author upon the properties of our abstract ideas and of those of mixed and simple modes, relatively to representative memory, on the methods suitable to make that kind of memory arise, and on the quality of the languages which favor it; in short on the means of making the word, the idea, and the fact always reciprocally support each other and be united in an indissoluble bond in our mind; for that is what we must attain. This chapter is very interesting and is not susceptible of extracts; it is necessary to read it.

After having spoken of memory in general and of its different kinds and of the modifications that it receives from continual use of artificial signs, it was very necessary to show the influence of these same signs and of their frequent repetition upon our judgments and to show how we are led to give, without our being aware, a kind of occult virtue to the signs of our ideas and a real existence outside ourselves to everything that is found clothed with a sign in our memory. This prejudice—almost invincible and inherent in human nature—is due to the reunion of the three causes: the direct effects of habit upon our judgments, the nature of the signs and of the associated ideas, and the forms of language.

Our first signs are connected with real and sensible objects; when we unite them to intellectual objects, we are led to regard these objects as if they were as real as the first.

We are accustomed to feel and see real and sensible objects existing outside of us; soon we also report as outside of us these intellectual objects which we judge equally real. This gives them a new character of existence.

Finally we are brought to this also by the forms of language. When we have personified them by a sign, they become the subjects of our propositions, the bearers of many qualities; they speak, they act, they are modified. All that we say of them is so many personifications which cannot fail to make them quite real for us, as soon as the memory that we have of them ceases a moment being fully representative and tends to become purely sensory or purely mechanical. But how difficult it is when it is a question of ideas of mixed modes which are formed of so many heterogeneous elements, of which it is very difficult not to let many escape, or when it is a matter of judgments whose proof we have forgotten, if it ever existed in our heads and the evidence of which is consequently no longer an affair of consciousness for us but only of reminiscence! Then as our author so forcibly says, everything is in the power of the *word*.

Such are the principal causes of the sinister power of words

and of our truly fanatical attachment for the apparent sense
of certain expressions which in truth have no real sense. But
if the sway of words is such over our judgments, how much
greater must it be over those series of judgments which we call
reasonings where all the inconveniences must be multiplied by
reason of the number of intellectual operations which are
united together or succeed one another. Here the uncertainty
of the human mind and its ease in going astray become truly
dreadful, and they are derived from the same source to which
it owes all its progress, from habit, that so essential part of
its nature, which constitutes all that it is. Our author, in his
last chapter, gives us on these dangers and on the means of
keeping clear of them, the finest ideas, which unfortunately
we cannot transfer to this extract. Let us limit ourselves to
concluding with him that, although calculation and reasoning
are absolutely the same operation, it is only in computation,
in the combination of ideas of quantity, that we may without
danger employ purely mechanical methods and with impunity
neglect ideas in order to be concerned only with signs, because
in computation one is concerned only with ideas of one and the
same kind; but in all other deductions in which all kinds of
ideas always enter, nothing enables us to dispense with the
duty of continually restoring the sign to its representative
faculty, for fear that the true representation will elude us.
We must always, as he has said, bear at the same time the
double burden of the sign and the idea for fear that the connection will be broken, and any project of a method tending
to rid us of this obligation, such as the *universally applicable
symbolism* of Leibnitz or others similar, is a pure chimera.
That is why mathematical combinations exact less power of
mind and should make the greatest progress; and why for other
kinds of research there is only a certain degree of habit in our
judgments which is really useful. When these judgments are
not sufficiently habitual, the mind is distracted by the feeling
of difficulty that it experiences. When they are too habitual,
their excessive facility hinders them from being conscious of

the elements which they include. These last words are in a nut shell all the effects of habit upon our intellectual operations. Let us observe, in ending, that this last chapter seemed to us the most satisfactory and the most enlightening of the whole work, and let us add in its praise that when the end of his race has come and his subject becomes more extended and more complicated an author appears most sure in his progress and most master of his subject, it is because he has well chosen his point of departure. This interesting memoir is terminated by an excellent summary, which should not be read first and by itself, for, not presenting the picture of the elements which it subsumes, it would offer only signs which might not be understood, or, in order to express this effect in the style of the author, it would give ground for the exercise of mechanical memory, but not representative.

Such, citizens, is the *précis* of the memoir which we propose that you crown. You will doubtless find much to be desired in this analysis; but, once more, works on these matters if they are well done are not susceptible of being condensed and it is impossible in a report to present the ideas of the author completely. The committee has not pretended to pronounce on all the points of the author's theory; it did not even think that it could not further add new improvements to his manner of presenting it; but it considered that this work was full of shrewdness and rich in acute and profound observations, that it betokened much knowledge and talent, that it threw great light upon the subject, and that it was very capable of causing new advance to be made in science. For all these reasons, it regards it as a very remarkable and very useful work.

MAINE DE BIRAN

THE INFLUENCE OF HABIT ON THE FACULTY OF THINKING

———

A work which obtained the prize on the question proposed by the Class of Moral and Political Sciences of the *Institut National:* namely,

To Determine What is the Influence of Habit Upon the Faculty of Thinking; or, in Other Words, to Show the Effect which the Frequent Repetition of the Same Performances Produces on Each of our Intellectual Faculties.

———

What are all the operations of the soul, if not movements and *repetitions* of movements?—Bonnet (*Psychologie*).

But after Condillac had broken down our ideas into the sensory elements which gave rise to them, the problem arose as to how they were combined into new syntheses. It was clear, for instance, that such phenomena as abstract or general ideas, and as the association of ideas in memory, could not be explained by the soul's activity, for the Condillacist technique eliminated the possibility of the soul's doing anything. Its function was to be done unto. Similarly the soul's activity could not be invoked to explain why a given sensation might now be remembered, now forgotten, now judged as this or that, now be seen to be brighter or duller than another. Rousseau and his school, who were anti-sensationalistic, used the soul whenever an agent of any kind was needed. But Condillac's technique required explaining all such functions as due to the inherent characteristics of the sensations themselves.

What then were the inherent characteristics of the sensations?

Sensations were first, of course, specific, differing in red from blue or a color from a sound. Each was itself. But at the same time each was not entirely of its own; it was more or less similar to other sensations. In the third place it had an affective coefficient, being either agreeable or disagreeable. And finally it had a certain duration, appearing and, after a certain lapse of time, disappearing. Condillac argued that a sensation appears to the subject in consciousness as of a certain kind, as like or unlike another, as long or brief, as agreeable or disagreeable. From these traits he hoped to be able to derive our so-called "mental faculties." Thus specificity would account for "attention," similarity or dissimilarity for judgment, the affective coefficient for desire and aversion and in the long run for volition, duration for memory and the sense of time.

But of these faculties desire alone could arise from a single sensation. All the others demanded at least two sensations, for they were all relational in their nature. Even duration

THE AUTHOR'S PREFACE

However encouraging and honorable may be the commendations of the Class which has awarded a prize to this Memoir, I confess, nevertheless, that I am only determining to publish it with that feeling of diffidence and fear so natural to an author who, without having put his powers to the test, submits himself for the first time to the severe and always formidable judgment of the public.

When I began this Memoir I did not think that it was destined to see the light of day: without aspiring to literary glory, I wished only to occupy the leisure of my retirement and to use for the study of my inner self the time that the particular circumstances in which I was placed, added to poor health, did not permit me to utilise in any other way.

In noting down the observations which I made upon myself, I was seeking at that time particularly to attain a greater degree of self-knowledge: I seemed to be writing only for myself. When I afterwards determined to offer the tribute of my reflections to the learned society which furnished me with their subject, I still thought that, in order to be perfectly understood, it sufficed to understand myself thoroughly. I neglected amplifications which would have been useless for learned judges and ornaments which would have been superfluous for severe ones. I started with principles agreed on among them, I spoke a language which was familiar to them; thus I had very rarely any need to offer proofs or definitions.

In addressing my work to the public, I now find myself in a far less favorable situation. I do not at all disguise what I have to fear—from the almost universal distaste which works of this kind inspire, when the severity of the subject is not tempered by agreeable forms of style; from the rigor with which people judge them, without being willing to take the necessary trouble to understand them; from the fashionable antipathy against what is called metaphysics; from the prejudices of some scholars who consider these sorts of researches useless, and from the opposition of enemies of philosophy, who would have them considered dangerous; in short, from the frivolous or bitter criticisms of some, as well as the serious accusations of others.

Doubtless, when the truth is sought sincerely with singleness of purpose, and when one has for oneself, besides an easy conscience, the approbation of a few wise and enlightened men, one can console oneself for all opposition; but perhaps it would be better still not to expose oneself to it.

I should at least have taken time to make the changes and corrections in this Memoir which it may need; to add in certain places the amplifications and explanations necessary to avert the danger of misinterpretation; in short, to give it a form which would put it within the reach of a greater number of readers.

Knowing, moreover, that a work of this kind is less deserving of regard for the correctness of its theory than for the practical utility of its applications, and convinced, also, that the whole art of education consists in forming good physical, intellectual and moral habits (that is to say, in perseveringly modifying man's organisation, mind and heart, in such a way, that he then directs himself towards all that is good and true, with that necessity, that sort of instinct, which is produced by a fortunate habit), I had thought of making the application of many principles scattered through this Memoir converge towards this great end, and of thus giving it as great a utility as the nature of the subject permits.

But, in following this plan, "I should be producing another work in place of the one which the approval of the Institute had just honored; I should be preventing myself from being able to reproduce it afterwards under such happy auspices. Besides, the Memoir judged by the Class, placed in the original in its archives, belongs to it in a way, and in presenting it as a prize work, it would not be proper for me to change the form of it.'' These arguments, made to me by persons whose friendship is very dear to me, and whose influence I am unable to resist, together with the interest which they have been pleased to take in the prompt printing of this Memoir, have overcome my repugnance and silenced all my objections.[1]

If I could flatter myself that I should find with the public the same leniency that I have obtained from my first judges, I should then be able to carry out with more assurance the plan that I have conceived: a second work, perhaps less imperfect, would again occupy or delight the leisure of my retirement; happy, after having completed it, to enjoy the pure and consoling idea of having been useful, of having acquired perhaps some right to the esteem of my fellow-men, if not by my success, at least by my efforts.

---

[1] I need to warn the reader that many notes scattered through this work and especially those in which I speak of scholars, whose ideas I have sometimes borrowed, have been added only since the printing of the memoir and in accordance with the judgment of the Institute. *Influence de l'habitude* (Heinrichs, Year XI).

Catching it Biran's answer to the question was based upon the principles of Cabanis; but, like many another treatise in the history of philosophy, it rose so far above its bases that they were forgotten. Like destutt de Tracy, the inventor of the word "ideology" and the chief of the school it signifies, Biran based all the operations of the mind upon the "faculty of receiving impressions" (i.e., sensory impressions). But all impressions are both active and passive: though is, each is now aroused by a cause external to the individual, now by the individual himself. Passive impressions he calls "sensations," active, "movements," acknowledging his debt to Tracy in making this distinction. But, though Tracy had made the required distinction, what he did not see was that practically each type of impression could be active as well as passive. In sight there is active touch—"feeling"—as well as passive touch—the "feel" of things: looking as well as seeing; listening as well as hearing; savoring as well as tasting. Only smelling is inactive, "its absolute immobility shows how passive it is," several odors mixed together blend into one despite the efforts of our attention. All we can do to modify it is to inhale slowly. Its very name, "scent," is properly used as a synonym for "sensing," for it is almost purely sensitive, excelled only by the somatic impressions which are the limit of sensation.

From the differences which there are in the degree of sensitivity (passivity) as contrasted with mobility (activity), Biran hoped to show that the power of perception, or of distinguishing our impressions from one another, did not depend upon our sensitivity, but upon our mobility. But since mobility was for him voluntary effort, it was clear that our power of perception was not a "transformed sensation" in the Condillacist manner, but an effect of something "internal" to the individual.

The rest of the essay is a detailed study of the effects of habit upon our various sensations and movements and upon our "determinations." These latter are the changes which linger on in our minds after the experience of an impression. They are for him both passive and active, simple memory and deliber

INTRODUCTION

"No one reflects about habit," a celebrated man has said (Mirabeau, *Conseils à un jeune prince*, etc.). Nothing is truer or better expressed than this short sentence. Reflection, in the physical as in the moral sense, requires a point of support, a resistance: but the most common effect of habit is to take away all resistance, to destroy all friction. It is like a slope on which one slides without perceiving it, without thinking of it.

Reflect upon what is habitual! . . . . who could or would wish to begin such reflection? How should one suspect some mystery in what one has always seen, done, or felt? About what should one inquire, should one be in doubt, should one be astonished? Heavy bodies fall, movement is communicated; the stars revolve over our heads; nature spreads out before our eyes her greatest phenomena: and what subject for wonder, what subject of inquiry could there be in such familiar things? And our own existence? the phenomena of sensibility, of thought? This host of modifications which succeed each other, of performances which repeat each other and accumulate since the beginning? this *me*, which escapes itself in the apparent simplicity and the extreme facility of its own acts, which ceaselessly eludes itself and is everywhere present to itself . . . how should one *reflect* on its habits, the most intimate, the most profound of all?

The first step of reflection is in everything the most difficult: it belongs only to the genius to take it. As soon as the great man who has the power to wonder, looks outside of himself, the veil of habit falls, he finds himself in the presence of nature, questions her freely, and receives her answers; but if he seeks to concentrate his gaze on himself, he remains still in the presence of habit, which continues to veil the composition

47

and the number of its products, as it at first concealed even their existence.

The first glance which we cast on our inner life reveals to us, in fact, nothing, so to say, except masses. It is the very picture of chaos. All the elements are confused; impressions, movements, operations, that which comes from without, that which is proper to the individual, all is mingled and combined in a single resultant, infinitely complex product, about which habit makes us think or feel as if it were simple. No beginning, no propagation, no succession; it is a circle which revolves on itself with an extreme rapidity. We do not distinguish the points through which it passes, we hardly know whether it does revolve.

When a first reflection has discovered a compound and when a beginning at analysis has separated it into its grossest parts, this analysis still stops at masses, as at the last terms of possible decomposition. If it seeks to advance, it still finds in habit even more opposition, more illusions and more errors.

It was, then, one and the same cause which assigned the last place in the order of human knowledge to the science of our ideas and in this science itself to the discovery of its primary and real elements. Thus the art of reasoning was known, its different forms were analysed, its methods were practiced with success in many ways, while the immediate products of sensitivity, the simplest results of the exercise of the senses, the evident origin of every faculty remained forgotten, unperceived, hidden by their simplicity, their very familiarity; so true is it that the slowness and difficulty of our knowledge are almost always proportionate to our proximity and intimacy with its objects, to the frequency or the constancy of the impressions that they occasion in us.

Analysis had perhaps already worn out its own instruments against the accumulations of habit, when it fortunately thought of reaching the same goal by an opposite road, as the chemist puts together, by the power of his skill, a compound like the one which he could not dissolve, but of which he surmised the elements. Observant metaphysicians, turning back to very simple hypotheses or to primitive facts which lay beyond the sphere of habit, endeavored out of these to reconstitute or to imitate its products in order to know them. In the degree in which they combined the elements of their creation, they compared the properties of their hypothetical results with the real complex products, and measured exactly in their own work proportions which they would never have been able to recognize in the working of habit. It is thus that they really succeeded in reflecting on habit. It is thus that the faculties and the operations of the understanding are little by little distinguished and emerge from chaos: but the roundabout way in which genius was obliged to proceed proves what were the difficulties of the work and the power of the cause that it was necessary to combat.

Sensible indeed of its powers were those first masters, who, turning against the bent of habit, found the origin of our faculties and the order of their genesis, which it had obscured or confused: those philosophers have still better appreciated its potency who have enlarged the territory of science and penetrated further into the secrets of thought. Are not all their discoveries so many victories snatched from habit, so many proofs of what it can do—as much to extend our faculties, to perfect and complicate our operations, as to veil the exercise of them? What is lacking now to determine precisely this general cause of our progress on the one hand, of our blindness on the other? What is there still to discover about a subject which has given impetus to so many researches, to so many imposing works? In short, after the masters, what remains to be said? The manner in which their work has been begun and continued may furnish us with some indications in regard to this.

In studying and recomposing the human understanding, it is necessary first to assure oneself of the nature, the number and the kind of materials which co-operate to form it. Doubtless, this important and laborious research does not permit one to observe at the same time how, in what order, and through what sequence of acts, these different elements could have been reunited, what was, as it were, the power of aggregation, the degree of persistency which each of them enjoyed, either by its own nature or by the frequency of its repetitions.

In inquiring into the genesis of our faculties, the analysts attempted first to know how they all arose from a primary faculty which by its transformation gave rise to the others; but, preoccupied with the line of descent of these powers from one another, those who investigated them were not able to examine with enough detail what was the mode of the individual development of each; what were the effects of the repetition of their exercise, whether these effects were constant and variable; how sensation (by hypothesis, a single faculty) could in being repeated, now be obscured, weakened or magnified, now be clarified, be distinguished, or remain in the same state; how habit could thus be now a force making for improvement, now a cause of deterioration; how, in short, the likeness or unlikeness of results, in the action of a single cause, could throw a new light on the origin of the faculties themselves, and show the bonds which unite them, as well as the differences which separate them.

The influence which habit exerts upon the faculty of thinking is, therefore, still an important question, susceptible of being considered from many new points of view. In order to treat it with all the exactitude desirable, it would perhaps be necessary to transport oneself to the point from which the creators of the science set out, to follow them in their journey, to reconstitute with them all those habits of which our understanding is composed, while insisting on various considerations which they have been forced to omit. This plan would be too great for my limited powers. But the philosophers who proposed the problem also took the measure of its extent; it is they who have brought it, in a manner, to its point of maturity; they have furnished its *data* and prepared for its solution. If the solution which I shall attempt to give is a good one, it is to them that the credit is due; the errors alone, if there be such, will come exclusively from myself.

The enunciation of the question presupposes as known the *faculties* and *operations* of the understanding; and, in fact, it is necessary to know the nature, the number, the interdependence or the mutual subordination, either of the faculties among themselves, or of the operations considered in relation to the faculties, in order to determine how the repetition of the action of some can influence others, or modify them. The solution is even implicitly contained in these real or supposed data. It must, therefore, emerge from discussing them and serve directly for their greater clarification—must strengthen them as principles, confirm or correct them as hypotheses.

It is with this object that I thought it needful to recall, at first separately, and to include in this Introduction, all that I have gathered, either from the works of my masters or from my own reflections, concerning the analysis of our intellectual faculties; and since it is well recognized that they are all derived from that of sensation, or of receiving impressions, I am going to attempt first of all to distinguish carefully the specific characteristics of these various impressions, in other words, to study the different ways in which we are sensible. I shall deduce from that the distinctions between the several faculties and the order of distribution of my subsequent inquiries. I ask pardon for the details into which I am about to go. They will, doubtless, at first appear very minute, but perhaps in the end they will be deemed to have been not altogether useless.

N. B.—Before going further, I have one more favor to ask of the reader, namely, to fix very deeply in his mind that, in all that is to follow, I have no object except to investigate and analyse *effects*, such as it is given us to know, on the one hand, by reflecting on that which we experience in the exercise of our senses and our different faculties, and on the other, by studying the conditions or the action of the organs on which this exercise appears to depend. I wanted to try to unite, at least in

certain respects, ideology and physiology. I was led to this
by the nature of the question, which belongs at the same time
to two sciences. I even thought that ideology in general
could only gain by this alliance; and that it belonged especially
to physical science to shed a little light on some obscurities of
the thinking being. But, once the physicial scientist's procedure is adopted, one is bound, following his example, to
concern oneself only with the relation and the succession of
phenomena, leaving behind one, and under the veil that covers
them, first causes which can never become for man objects
of *knowledge*.

We know nothing of the nature of *forces*. They are manifested to us only through their effects. The human mind
observes these effects, follows the thread of their diverse
analogies, calculates their relations when they are susceptible
of measurement: such are the limits of its power.

To study only in inner reflection and in the results (known
or supposed) of the action of the organs, what metaphysics
has long sought in the nature of the soul itself, is, therefore,
to abandon a *cause*, of which we knew only the name, in order
to hold to the facts of experience and observation, which
belong to our own domain. It is to apply directly to ideology
the excellent philosophical method practiced with so much
success in all subjects by the fine minds and geniuses who honor
our century.

The examples of Condillac and Bonnet especially[1] which I
like to cite, and which have often served me as models, prove
that physics can be carried over into metaphysics, without
damage to anything respected or really deserving of respect—
without shaking any hope, or attacking any of those consoling
opinions which serve to supplement the fragile happiness of
life and often protect against vice and encourage to virtue.
But, as Bonnet himself so forcefully says in his preface to the

[1] See what Condillac says, particularly in his *Logique*, Chapter IX, first
part, on the physics of memory, of the conservation of ideas and of habits;
Bonnet, in his *Psychologie* and the *Essai analytique de l' âme*.

Essai analytique: "Would virtue lose its value in the eyes of philosophy, if it should be proved that it depends upon some fibres of the brain?"

I. The faculty of receiving impressions is the first and the most general of all those which are manifested in the organic living being.

It embraces them all: we cannot conceive any of them as existing before it or without it, nor any which is not more or less closely dependent on it. The exercise of this faculty varies differently in each organ in correlation either with its characteristic structure or with the nature and manner of acting of the objects to which it is appropriate. There are, therefore, as many classes of impressions as there are senses or organs capable of receiving them.

Each of these classes could be related to particular faculties (as people sometimes, in fact, speak of the faculty of touch, sight, hearing, etc.) and this distinction of the faculties would perhaps be better justified as there are many operations which sometimes depend on the exercise of an isolated sense alone, or of two together, without having anything in common with the others which have also their particular functions, essentially distinct. The functions of instinct, for example, are not performed by the same organs as those of knowledge. But metaphysicians investigating in our organs the common property of receiving impressions, and in the individual that of being affected or modified by them, grouped all the results whatsoever of the exercise of the senses under the generic name of *sensations;* and the faculty of receiving or experiencing sensations was called the faculty of feeling, or *physical sensitivity.*

This word *feeling* has accordingly been extended to all that we can experience, perceive or know, in ourselves or outside of ourselves, by the action of external objects, as well as independently of this action, in such a way that it has become synonymous with that other word *consciousness,* used by the early metaphysicians to designate the sort of inward vision through which the individual perceives what happens within himself.

Let us notice that the expression *feeling*, in taking on this width of meaning, has no less kept its proper and vulgar signification, which is applied especially to affective modifications. Hence the same word is often used in a double sense, and perhaps a certain ambiguity colors the first principles of the science.

If one, in fact, uses the same term *sensation* to express now a simple affective modification, now a product composed of an impression, a movement, an operation, etc., is it not to be feared that the identity of expression will often serve to confuse things quite different and to confirm illusions to which we are already sufficiently inclined?

If one subsumes under a single term the diverse products of the action of different organs before determining the specific characters of each, how shall one then distinguish the subsequent operations of thought which can only be founded on the difference of these products? It is this last reason especially which has induced me to undertake a somewhat detailed analysis of our sensory impressions and to arrange them in two separate classes.

II. I separate all our impressions into those which are *active* and those which are *passive*. In order to eliminate the difficulties to which these old denominations might give rise, let us note at once the ground of my distinction: When I experience a pain or a titillation in some internal part of the body, and in general a feeling of well-being or uneasiness, when I am hot or cold, when an agreeable or disagreeable odor pursues me, I say that I feel, that I am modified in a certain way; it is evident to me that I exercise no power on my modification, that I have no means at hand to interrupt or to change it; I say, therefore, once more that I am or that I feel myself to be in a *passive* state. I can, indeed, know by reasoning that what I experience is not at all a mechanical result of the action exercised on my organs or of a simple communication of movements submitted to necessary, fixed, invariable laws as the impact of body on body; that there is a real action peculiar to the sensitive organ which is directed in accordance with particular laws and gives the tone rather than receives it. . . . But this purely internal occurrence is executed in me without my agency, and, in considering the phenomenon only in the light of the knowledge that I have of it, it seems to me that I would not be otherwise modified, even if my organs were passively submitted to the impulse which stirs them. If there is then, as one cannot doubt, a *sensitive* activity, I will distinguish it from *motor* activity which alone I will call "activity," because it is manifest to my inner sense with the greatest clearness.

If, in fact, I move one of my limbs or if I go from one place to another, abstracting any other impression than the one which results from my own movement, I am modified in a very different way from what I was before. First, it is indeed *I* who create my modification. I can begin it, suspend it, vary it in every way, and the consciousness that I have of my activity is for me as evident as the modification itself.

When I am limited to purely *affective* sensations, if one of them becomes vivid enough to occupy my entire faculty of feeling, I identify myself with it. I do not separate my existence from it. It seems to me that my *ego* is concentrated in one point. Time and space have disappeared, I make neither distinctions nor comparisons.

When I move, my being is extended outward; but, always present to itself, it recovers itself, it apprehends itself successively or at once in many points. Each movement, each step made is a very distinct modification which affects me doubly —by itself and by the act which determines it. It is *I* who move, or who *wish* to move, and it is also *I* who am moved. Those are, indeed, the two terms of the relation which are necessary for the foundation of this first simple judgment of personality, *I am.* I do not believe that one could recognize the same basis in absolutely passive impressions, but this delicate point can be clarified elsewhere, at least as far as it is susceptible of clarification.

We can already begin to perceive that activity, as that which is distinctive of the ego and its ways of being, is directly attached to the faculty of *moving*,[2] which ought to be distinguished from that of *feeling*, as a main branch is distinguished from the trunk of the tree, or rather as twin trees are distinguished which cling together and grow into one.

But such is the nature of our organization, such is the direct correspondence, the intimate connection which exists between the two faculties of feeling and moving, that there is almost no impression which does not result from their mutual co-operation and which is not consequently active in one situation and passive in another.

Take away the particular modification that results from the exercise of our power of locomotion and what we experience in unusual affections of the internal organs, and we shall find that all other sense impressions have a mixed character and that sensory and motor action, feeling and movement, are there combined, in very different proportions, it is true, now one predominating over the other, now it in its turn subordinated, with finally both seeming to keep between them the most perfect equilibrium.

When feeling predominates up to a certain point, the movement which occurs with it is as nothing, since the individual has no consciousness of it, and the impression remains passive. I shall keep for all impressions of this sort the name of *sensations*. If movement takes the upper hand and, in some way,

---

[2] Citizen Destutt-Tracy is the first who has clearly connected the origin of knowledge, of the distinction of our ways of being, and of the ego which experiences them, in short of the judgment of *real existence* and of all the other judgments which are derived from it, with the faculty of moving and with voluntary *activity*. (See the *Mémoires de la classe des sciences morales et politiques*, 1st vol., year IV, and especially the *Eléments d'idéologie* which I regret having known too late and not until my memoir was almost entirely finished.) I have merely developed the principal ideas of this admirable philosophy, by seeking in the impressions and the play of each organ separately, the effects of this cause or active faculty, of which he had already appreciated the general influence in the formation of our ideas and the production of our knowledge.

the initiative, or even if it is so balanced with sensitivity that it is not eclipsed by it, the individual is active in his impression. He perceives the part that he plays in it, distinguishes it from himself, can compare it with others, etc. I shall call any impression which will have these characteristics *perception*.

Let us now examine the exercise of each of our senses. What is, so to say, the part played by feeling and what by movement? 1. The organ of touch first offers us the two faculties perfectly combined, but easy to recognize and to distinguish.

If one places on my hand an object whose surface is rough or smooth, mildly warm or biting cold, etc., as long as the contact lasts I experience an agreeable or painful impression, which it is not at all within my power to augment, to diminish, or to stop in any way. That is the part of feeling. Even if the motor faculty were paralyzed, it would act in the same way. It is to sensations of this sort that touch would be limited if it were not endowed with mobility, in which case it would be inferior to many other parts of the body, which are covered by skin but whose sensitivity is much nicer and more delicate.

In these passive impressions, generally confused, in which it is very difficult to distinguish the degrees and the nuances, which are elusive even in my present condition and with all my acquired experience, I see nothing which could enable one to distinguish the *ego* from its modifications, nor its modifications from each other, if they were isolated.

If the object is left on my hand, supposing it to have a certain weight, it occasions in me a modification of a very different sort. I feel my hand pushed down and dragged along by a force opposed to mine. Surely that which pushes my hand, or which constrains the movement which tends to raise or to hold back my arm, is not the *ego*. If I were reduced to this impression alone, I should know that there was something outside of me which I distinguish and compare, and all the sophisms of idealism could not shake this conviction.

If—the object still remaining on my hand—I wish to close the hand, and if, while my fingers are folding back upon themselves, their movement is suddenly stopped by an obstacle on which they press and which thwarts them, a new judgment is necessary; *this is not I*. There is a very distinct impression of solidity, of resistance, which is composed of a thwarted movement, of an *effort* which I make, in which I am *active*, and of many more or less affective modifications, corresponding to those which are called tactile qualities (smooth, rough, cold or hot) which I can in no wise affect.

Let us stop an instant on this impression of *effort* which comes from any thwarted movement. We must learn to know it well.

Effort necessarily entails the perception of a relation between the being who moves, or who wishes to move, and any obstacle whatsoever which is opposed to its movement; without a *subject* or a will which determines the movement, without a something which resists, there is no *effort* at all, and without effort no knowledge, no perception of any kind.

If the individual did not *will* or was not determined to begin to move, he would know nothing. If nothing resisted him, he likewise would know nothing, he would not suspect any existence; he would not even have an *idea* of his own existence. If the movement having begun should stop at the first resistance (for example, if, when an object is placed on his hand, his fingers, in closing, should stop at the slightest contact), the individual would simply know that an obstacle exists; but in no way whether this obstacle is absolutely impenetrable, solid, hard or soft, etc. These properties of matter can only be manifest to him in so far as he *wills* to continue the movement and it is the intensity of his effort which is their gauge. If he presses the obstacle with all his might without being able to close his hand, he has a fixed limit which makes him conscious of impenetrability and hardness. If the obstacle yields more or less easily, he has a measure of its different degrees of softness, flexibility, etc.

The individual, therefore, is only aware of his most elementary relation to external existence in so far as he begins to move, and of the other relations which follow in so far as he wishes to continue the movement. But if we suppose that resistance diminishes progressively to the point of becoming insensible, the last termination of decreasing effort will be the limit and, as it were, the vanishing-point of all perception, of all knowledge.

What we have just said of *restrained* movement applies likewise to *free* movement; the perception of the latter is equally rooted in effort, which exerts itself in proportion to the different degrees of resistance which the muscles oppose to the will. As muscular inertia diminishes, as effort or the motor impression itself weakens and ends by disappearing, the movement is executed without consciousness, without will.

It is thus evident, first, that the impression of effort is susceptible to a multitude of nuances—from its maximum, which corresponds to an insurmountable, impenetrable obstacle, down to the least degree of muscular resistance; second, that as long as this impression lingers, there is always a perceived relation between the self which wills and the obstacle which resists—such being the origin and the ultimate foundation of every known relation to the external world; third, that the obstacle being fixed, the effort depends upon the will, but that when the resistance diminishes to the vanishing point, effort and will vanish with it.

The reflections which we have just made upon touch considered in this particular context, apply in general to all our motor organs. Coming back now to the impressions characteristic of this sense, let us examine how the two faculties of feeling and moving work together to produce them.

By movement alone we could scarcely know anything more than differently resisting masses; the hand, one might say, decomposes these masses, lays bare their elements, distinguishes their properties, makes clear their subtle differences: it is the foremost instrument of analysis and all its advantages evidently depend upon its construction—upon the superior mobility of its parts and the very nature of their sensitivity.

In virtue of their mobility, the fingers close, adjust themselves upon the solid object, grasp it in several points simultaneously, go over each of its surfaces one by one, glide lightly over its framework, and follow the guidance of its structure. Thus resistance, although one, separates itself into many distinct impressions: the surface is abstracted from the solid, the contour from the surface, the line from the contour; each perception is complete in itself and yet the whole which they compose is perfectly determined.

Sensitivity gathers together the discoveries of movement as they are made, catches the most delicate nuances and takes possession of them. It apprehends this imperceptible ridge, these little eminences, these prominences, which disappear in the total resistance or in the rapidity of the movement, and draws with exactitude what the motor organ could only sketch, as it were, if one should suppose it callous. It is thus, in fact, that the blind geometer owes the niceness and the number of the perceptions which he forms of the modes of figured extension as much to the delicacy of the feeling of the receptors (*houppes nerveuses*) as to the agility and flexibility of his fingers.

Moreover, have not the extreme division and the prodigious number of nerve fibres which excite the muscles of touch, equally for their object the discrimination and the precision of movements and the variety and the nicety of sensations? Are not all these characteristics connected with the same fundamental, organic condition? The more attenuated nerves must receive the less confused vibrations and transmit to the cerebral organ the finer currents (*les avertissements plus détaillés*). If these nerves have a covering of such a nature as to moderate their sensitivity without dulling it, the contact appropriate to this mode of sensitivity will not excite it enough to counteract the products of the concurrent motor activity. Thus the two functions of the organ will be in that degree of balance which helps to determine every distinct perception.

Let us observe, in support of the preceding, that if sensitivity becomes predominant, if the tactile qualities stimulate, irritate or repel the nervous extremities too much, then voluntary action, i.e., effort, diminishes. Affective modification alone remains and the perception of forms is confused and later lost to memory.

It is only, therefore, as a motor organ that touch contributes essentially to putting the individual in communication with external nature; it is because it combines the two faculties in the most exact proportion that it is susceptible of such nice, such detailed, such persistant impressions; in short, it is in virtue of this that it opens a feeding ground for intellect and furnishes it with its more substantial nourishment.

It is customary to compare the different sense impressions with those of touch proper. All our sensations, it is said, are only a kind of touch. That is very true if one thinks only of their sensory or passive function; but with respect to activity and movement, no other sense organs are similar. Only in proportion to their mobility are they more or less capable of corresponding to or of coöperating with touch, of profiting by its warnings and of associating their impressions with it. We shall make this clear in a rapid analysis of the senses.

2. The organ of sight is the one which is endowed with the most delicate sensitivity. It is exposed to the contact of light in comparative nakedness. The fibrils of the retina, in a state of division which thought can scarcely grasp, are suited to the rarity of the fluid which strikes them. The colors and all their gradations seem to be painted on the sensitive canvas with the finest, lightest brush. All seems arranged to transmit directly to the cerebral center distinct impressions, which appear by their very nature to be the determining power of its activity.

Nevertheless, it is difficult to say in what narrow limits the functions of sight would be circumscribed if we did away with the mobility peculiar to this organ and especially with its association and close correspondence with touch.

The visual impression, or at least its complement, depends upon the motive activity, which occurs with it and prepares it.

By a strictly muscular action and with an effort doubtless very perceptible in the beginning, the eye is fixed, directed, opened more or less wide, its diameter is contracted or enlarged to make the rays converge at the proper point, to temper their strength or fortify their weakness. It executes this multitude of movements necessary for apprehending objects, for distinguishing tints, for making these shapes its own, which touch—first in action and superior in mobility—analyses for it and with it.

But would the results of this activity which is characteristic of and very marked in the organ of sight, be nothing if they were isolated? When the individual opens or closes his eyes, he creates or annihilates his modifications and can vary them in many ways.

We do not begin to know up to what point these experiments could be carried on or what would be the results of them; but would there not be at least some colors distinguished from others, an acting *ego*, distinct from the modifications which it helps produce, a perceived effort of which the subject and the object could not be confused? That suffices, it seems to me, to destroy the parallel, which has sometimes been made, between the impressions proper to sight and those of the passive senses: if one could suppose an individual limited to these first impressions, he would do more than feel, he would perceive, because he would move. It is only because of its mobility that the eye maintains such intimate relations with touch[3] and associates its operations so closely with it. Now, it is incontestible in all hypotheses that this alliance must change the inherent character of visual impressions, increase their activity and their persistence, render judgment more fixed and effort more distinct, since external resistance is substituted for simple muscular resistance or coincides with it in the beginning.

This leads us to make an important remark, the application of which will soon be seen: namely, that a slightly mobile

---

[3] How could the hands say to the eyes: *Do as we do*, if the eyes were immovable? (See Condillac's *Traité des Sensations*.)

organ, which, if isolated, allows only more or less passive and confused impressions, can acquire the activity which it lacks, by its association or correspondence with an organ superior in mobility.

For that matter, we can apply to sight almost all that we have said of touch. In the natural state and in the ordinary exercise of the organ, the two functions—sensory and motor—correspond with and balance each other with no mutual disturbance; but if, by the object's manner of acting or the disposition of the sense organ, the impressions should become too vivid, the affective effect would arise alone or be dominant and the individual would no longer perceive.

3. The vibrations, communicated by the resonant object either to the air or perhaps to a more subtle fluid, are transmitted at first to the auditory organ and through it (or sometimes even without this intermediary) stimulate the nervous system more or less. The more delicate and mobile the nervous system is, the greater the affective force of the impressions; the more passive the individual is in receiving them, the less distinct they are.

We see very sensitive people who are affected by a series of sounds much as by an unpleasant noise. It is also true of the *timbre* of instruments, such as the *harmonica*,[4] which excite sensation in a high degree, that the more one *feels* the effects of them, the less one *perceives* them.

In order that sounds can be distinguished, it is first necessary that the vibrations be communicated with a moderate degree of force in a certain order, following certain determined proportions, to the fibres of the spiral lamina, the structure of which indeed appears highly appropriate for the discrimination of harmonious and melodious series.

But is this discrimination related only to the sensibility of the organ, to its passive functions? Our preceding remarks prove the contrary. Furthermore, in order to hear well, it is

---

[4] Not the American instrument. Biran refers to an instrument made of a series of little bells or glass rods graduated in half tones.—Tr.

necessary to *listen*. Now, what is listening, if not putting into
action the muscles destined to communicate different degrees
of tension to the membrane of the tympanum, etc.? It is
true that here the effort has become imperceptible, that the
acting and the apparatus of movement, being quite internal,
do not manifest themselves at all as expressions of the will;
that the ear being in man externally immobile, open to all
impressions without direct means of avoiding or moderating
them, seems to be an organ whose passivity varies directly
with the predominance of its sensitivity. But nature herself
has taken care to supplement these faults; she has restored
equilibrium by associating in the most intimate way her passive
impressions with the activity of an organ essentially motor.

The sounds transmitted to the ear and through it to the
cerebral center, not only determine the action of its own
muscles, but even (and through the effect of a sympathy which
does not strike us at all, so close to us and habitual is it) the
movements of the vocal organ, which repeats them, imitates
them, turns them back, if one might say so, towards their
source, and afterwards makes these fleeting modifications enter
the sphere of the individual's activity, establishes them and
incorporates them there.

When we perceive sounds (and we always perceive the more
distinctly those which resemble the ones which we can make,
imitate or articulate ourselves), the vocal instrument there-
upon acquires determinations like those of hearing and, if one
might say so, rises to the same tone: on hearing singing or
speaking, we sing or speak under our breath. There is an
instinct of imitation still more noticeable here than in any other
movement; it carries us along generally without our awareness.

Thus, the individual who listens is himself his own echo.
The ear is as if instantaneously struck both by the direct
external sound and the internal sound reproduced. These
two imprints are added together in the cerebral organ, which
is doubly stimulated—both by the action which it communicates and by the action which it receives. Such is the cause

of *têtes sonores.*[5] That is the basis of all the characteristics of discrimination, of persistency and of recall, which auditory impressions enjoy in a high degree. . . . We could as well perhaps call them *vocal;* for if we speak because we hear, it is true to say that we only hear in as far as we speak; the two organs act and react upon each other incessantly. Nature itself seems to have preordained the modes of their mutual action in the different species (see Buffon, *Discours sur la nature des oiseaux*), almost always proportioning the acuteness and delicacy of the one to the strength and the pliableness of the other.

The association of the voice with hearing is analogous in its primary effects to that which exists between touch and sight. In both cases, it is the more highly mobile organ which communicates its activity to the one in which sensitivity predominates.

4. The sense of taste is the one which at first seems to be most closely related to touch; the tastes are in fact only the touch inherent in the tongue and the palate; sapid molecules are closely and directly applied to their nerve receptors as more material particles are applied to the surface of the hand and the ends of the fingers. Different tastes may be very well compared to the tactile sensations of cold, hot, pleasant, rough, prickling; similarly these two kinds of modifications have many names in common in our languages.

The tastes, generally as confused in the gradations which separate them as the separated tactile qualities of resistance and more variable and fleeting, have a much greater activity. In the exercise of passive touch the individual is modified, so to say, only in a *local* way; but in the exercise of taste, especially when it is effected by need, the sensation becomes almost general and very complex. An internal organ, which has the most extended influence on the sensitive system, plays the

[5] Literally "sonorous" or "resonant heads." M. Tisserand writes me that for Biran a *tête sonore* is a head in which occurs the inner speech which accompanies the idea. In speaking the thought to ourselves, the speech resounds in our head. It is what is now known in psychology as an auditory image.—Tr.

most direct part in it. Now, it is known how tumultuous, confused and passive all the affections are when these inner organs are directly concerned.

It is plain that, if the sensitive function becomes predominant in taste impressions, motor activity will be obscured in the same proportion. The organ of taste, which is at the same time that of speech, is endowed with a very great mobility. The effort which takes place in mastication or the pressure of the lips, teeth, palate against solid bodies, would doubtless be sufficient to give us more or less confused ideas of resistance and of some of its modes; many species of animals, as is known, have their touch in mouth and nose.

But in strictly tactile operations the perception of solidity and form is the end and purpose of the movement made. The impression of effort is alone or dominant; it is to it that everything is referred; it is not confused with any other. In the operation of taste, on the contrary, resistance is only accessory and movement is only a means. The *sensation* is the end and when it exists, it absorbs all that is not it. In touch, the resistance is fixed, the individual can at will prolong the tactile impression; in taste, this impression is only momentary and the sensation itself which follows it and effaces even the memory of it has no permanence. Either it is weak and disappears in the very effort which tries to seize it; or it is vivid and cancels or conceals this effort.

The individual who tastes with most attention is thus always more or less passive in what he experiences; he is not, as in perception properly so called, an agent and a reflecting, disinterested observer. Moreover, the sensations of taste always approach more and more the characters of perception (without ever, nevertheless, attaining the same degree of distinctness and persistency) in proportion as they are less affective, more separated from the activity of internal organs and more subordinated to the slow, voluntary, and prolonged movements of their own organ. Let us remark also that the tastes of solid bodies are more distinct in sense and a little less confused

in memory than those of liquids, which agrees very well with
our principles.

5. What we have just said of taste applies still more directly
to smell.   These two senses are closely connected with each
other as with their internal organs and their impressions
become only the more affective and the more confused.   Those
of smell especially are eminently adapted to the general sensitivity of the system.   This sense, first put into play by instinct,
remains almost entirely subordinated to it; its absolute immobility proclaims how passive it is and it might be said that it
holds among our external senses the same rank as the polyp
or the oyster in the scale of animal life.   Its functions, it is
true, are connected with the movement of respiration, but this
fundamental movement is of vital necessity, involuntary, continuous by its nature and for that very reason almost insensible.
Also odors are sensations *par excellence* as our very language
indicates;[6] they are the least discriminated from one another;
when many are united together, they fuse into a single sensation, which it is impossible for us to analyse, in spite of the
voluntary attention which we give to the combination.   Let
us notice that this attention consists only of the movement of
uniform, slow and prolonged inspiration.   That is the limit
of our power over these modifications.

6. Finally come the impressions internal to the body and
which might be called *pure sensations*.   Here the sensitive
function exists in absolute isolation.   No perceived effort, no
activity, no discrimination, no trace of memory, all light is
eclipsed with the faculty of movement.

Since in relating each class of impressions to its proper organ,
we constantly see the power of discrimination and perceptibility
decrease in the same proportion as on the one hand the sensitive capacity of these organs increases or is isolated and on the
other as their mobility diminishes, I think I can conclude with
enough certainty from the analyses which precede that the

---

[6] In French the word *sentir* may be used to mean both to *smell* and to *feel*
(i.e., to have a sensation).—Tr.

faculty of perceiving or of distinguishing our impressions from one another (after they are separated in some way from the ego which experiences them) is not at all an attribute of the purely sensitive being, but depends absolutely upon the faculty of voluntary motion with which it varies in all its phases. Consequently, perception is not at all a general operation which the individual can freely exercise on all kinds of modifications which he experiences or receives, but each class of impressions has its specific character which makes it adapted to perception or sensation. This character, moreover, depends first upon the form of the organ, upon the proportion in which feeling and movement can be combined in it. In the second place (these conditions being presupposed), it depends upon the type of the external stimulus, upon its degree of stimulating power, from which it follows further that an impression may be felt without being perceived and that one cannot say that one perceives a sensation. For example, if I touch a hot body, I perceive the solidity at the same time as I feel the heat, but I cannot say that I perceive this latter modification. In short, although I have made of the word *sensations* a generic term, it does not at all follow that one is authorized to attribute to some sensations what one says of others. This principle, for example, that the sensation is transformed to become such and such an operation of the understanding, would not be generally true at all; for there are sensations (to wit, all the impressions which we have called by that name) which are not transformed in any way, as we shall presently see, in deducing other consequenes from our premises.

III. The first action exercised by objects upon sentient organs or by motor organs upon objects is not limited to the effect of the moment. Any modification can only be the result of an alteration effected in the sense or in some center of the [sensory] system. Now, this alteration, which persists and more or less outlasts the impression, we call in general a *determination;* and as there are two classes of impressions, there are two sorts of determinations, the one for feeling and the other for movement. These determinations may be effectuated[7] equally by the renewed activity of the same causes which formed them or spontaneously, and in the absence of these causes, by virtue of a lively force inherent in the organs, when they have once been stimulated with objects. Let us examine what happens in these two different cases.

1. If the sensory determination is effectuated by the repeated stimulus of the same external cause, it can only result in a modification like the first, different merely in degree. Since the difference will be proportionate to the intensity and persistence of the first alteration effected in the organ, the renewed sensation will be in general weaker and less moving (*affective*).

The individual cannot perceive this difference without recognizing the sensation as being the same that had already affected him, and reciprocally he cannot recognize it without perceiving some difference. Now, if one made an abstraction from every external sign, from every circumstance associated with an affective modification, if one supposed an individual limited to different degrees of this modification or to several others of the same kind, is it likely that he would be able to appreciate gradations which always tend to be confused, even for us whose means of recognition are so multiplied, whose sensations and judgments are so indivisibly united? Is it in fact through the intrinsic characters of our pure sensations and by the alterations and deteriorations which they undergo that we succeed in distinguishing and recognizing them when they are renewed? Could we ever say whether such and such an internal pain, such and such a degree of cold or heat, is the same as that which we have already experienced or whether it is different from it?

Let us observe that the more our sensations are one or are freed from any associated states, the more they exclusively occupy our faculty of feeling and the less we are able to recog-

---

[7] I shall say that a determination is effectuated when the organ or the central nervous system is returned to the same condition in which it was by virtue of the original action.

nize them if they chance to be renewed. What then would be the case of a being who were absolutely identified with each of his modifications? In order to compare two manners of being or to perceive their difference it is necessary that the *ego* put itself, so to speak, outside of the one and the other alike: a judgment of personality is first necessary. Now, how could there be a judgment where there is only one term? To suppose that the *ego* is identified with all its modifications and nevertheless to suppose that it compares them and distinguishes them, is to make a self-contradictory supposition. Let us recognize, therefore, that in a renewed and weakened sensation considered by itself there is no foundation for remembrance.

Though the sensory determination were effectuated by the repeated action of the stimulus or spontaneously in its absence, the result would never be anything other than a more or less weakened modification, without relation to existence, cause or time. For one evidently cannot suppose these relations to exist without a distinct and prior personality. For the sentient being to be able to distinguish the memory of sensation, or to have within him the equivalent of what we call *memory*, it would be necessary for the *ego* as it is now modified to compare itself to the same *ego* modified at another time; it would be necessary, as Condillac has said, "that he should feel faintly what he has been at the same time that he feels vividly what he is." But is it the same thing to feel faintly as to feel that one has been? How can one find a temporal relation in this single circumstance of faintness? Is not a faint sensation *present* just as much as a vivid sensation?

Here we meet the same difficulties as we did in the case of memory.

2. The motor determination is a tendency of the organ or the motor center to repeat the action or the movement which has occurred for the first time. When this tendency passes from the *virtual* to the *actual*, as a result of renewed external stimulation, the individual wills and executes the same movement. He is conscious of a renewed effort. This renewed

effort differs from the first by a greater degree of facility. Now, this facility can be recognized and distinguished, because here are the elements of a relation, a subject which *wills*, always self-identical, and a variable term, *resistance*. As this subject and the variable term could not be identified in the original action, they will be still separate in the second, the third, etc., as long as the least resistance remains.

The motor being who has acted, and who acts now with greater facility, cannot perceive this difference without recognizing his own identity as *willing subject*. But this recognition necessarily entails that of the end of the action; they presuppose each other, and are closely united in the same impression of effort. It is obvious how easily memory can be explained in this manner; we shall see elsewhere how this judgment, starting from the origin which has just been assigned to it, is clarified and extended by the addition of new circumstances.

If the motor determination is effectuated spontaneously in the absence of the first cause, the individual wills the same action. He puts himself again, as far as he is able, in the same state in which he was while performing it when the first cause was present. He is conscious of the effort which he is again making. But as he distinguishes with the greatest clarity *free* movement from movement *opposed* by an obstacle, it will be impossible for him to confuse a memory with an impression, for example, the representation which is made in his brain of the form of a solid which he has touched, with the resistance which this solid if present would oppose to him.

When by virtue of the determination acquired by the sensory and motor center, the hand resumes or tends to resume the same position that it had in touching or in encircling a ball and the individual consequently finds himself again in almost the same active state in which he was, he *perceives;* he touches again, one might say, in thought, an absent ball.

This second perception, quite distinct from the first, is referred to it and implies it, as a copy (recognized as such) is referred to the original; it is this copy, thus conceived, that I call an *idea*.

Let us notice that the individual acts in the case of the representation, or the idea of the tangible solid, as he acted in the case of the direct impression; all that he has, so to speak, put of himself, in the latter, he puts, performs in the former. He would create, therefore, a second perception almost equal to the first and only different in degree, if he disposed of the sensation as he disposes of the movement; but while the hand acts in order to resume the form of the ball, the sensory extremities remain inactive, languid, and do not activate themselves at all at the pleasure of the will.   The same is true of ideas of sounds: when the vocal organ repeats or tends to repeat the movements which correspond to auditory impressions, the individual is as active in the idea as he was in the perception, and the difference would be insensible, if hearing could renew the *direct* sounds, as the voice reproduces reflected sounds.

We see clearly in these two examples that the production of ideas is only a result or a sequel of the activity of the impressions themselves.   Without this activity inherent in the character of the impressions, in the mobility of the organs which they concern or to which they are related, in a word, without motor determination (in which they may originate), there is neither memory nor ideas.

We may be confirmed in this partly by our daily experience; for the facility that we have in recognizing an object or in clearly recalling an idea of it, depends less on the affective force with which it has struck us than on the voluntary attention that we have given to it, attention which is always bound in its origin to some of the movements which we make.

The impression of effort, which is the common origin of our perceptions and our ideas, is susceptible of an infinity of gradations.   It is singularly weakened by repetition (of which we shall have below enough opportunities to be convinced). Now, although the activity of consciousness weakens in the same situations, its primary results do not at all follow the

same law of degradation. Impressions and ideas, to the origin
of which this activity contributed, remain distinct and outlast
it. This is particularly true of the representative functions of
the visual organ. These functions are actually executed with
such promptitude and facility that we no longer perceive the
voluntary action which directs them and we are absolutely
unaware of the source that they have in resistance. In the
same manner, therefore, as effort does not exist or is insensible
in visual perceptions, it will be equally so in the production of
ideas or corresponding *images*. These images will arise spontaneously in the organ of thought, will follow each other with
the greatest rapidity, will shine with the most vivid clearness,
will be eclipsed to reappear again and this without the will
of the individual seeming to participate in any way. *Visual
determinations*, therefore, approach through this last circumstance, those which we have distinguished under the name of
sensory; and one would perhaps be much more correct in
ranking them in the same class (if other characters did not
prevent) since the colors, identified by a primary habit with
perceptions of forms and figures, appear to be in some way the
natural excitants of the sensitivity proper to the cerebral
center, as their images are the most immediate products of its
activity. In all intensifying of this sensitivity, occasioned by
some unusual irritation in the brain's substance itself, there
arise ordinarily *visions* which strike the individual with as much
force as reality itself; and in the natural state how many
times does it not happen that these same images, taking the
ascendancy of direct perceptions, shut off all return to the model,
substitute themselves for it, and are confused with it, as
products of sensory determinations are confused with those of
the causes which formed them. Let us take note that these
illusions do not equally arise in ideas corresponding to active
impressions of touch or hearing.

These observations lead us to distinguish two different modes
of reproduction: the one, which is related to the different
ideas drawn from movement, from resistance and its forms,

from vocal sounds, is executed always with a more or less sensible voluntary effort; it is essentially accompanied by the judgment of *remembrance*.

The other, which is especially related to the production of *images*, is connected with remembrance only in a moderately lively degree and this liveliness itself depends upon the nature and the intensity of the organic causes which determine the spontaneous appearance of the images.

The first mode of reproduction is active. I will call it *recall*. The second is more or less passive; and because it is applied principally to visual images, I will call it *imagination*. The faculty of recall while acting and making an effort will be called *memory*. Let us add some more traits to the distinctive characters of these two faculties.

1. The voluntary movements which have formed the active impressions or coöperated essentially in making them distinct are still the sole means or subjects of recall. One can, therefore, say that they are the *signs* of the impressions which they distinguish and of the ideas which they recall; and this name of *signs* is so much the more justified in this circumstance since the movements, at the same time that they serve to put the individual again in a state in which he already has been and furnish thus a hold for his will, a *pou sto* for modifying himself, are still the only marks by which he can manifest externally this will and these inner modifications.

I shall, therefore, say that the movement or the effort reproduced in the hand, when it represents or tends to represent the solid, is the *sign* of the idea of form and external resistance.

Vocal movements will also be the signs of auditory impressions or their ideas. Those of mastication or of inspiration could be considered equally signs both of tastes and smells, if the predominance of sensitivity in these two sorts of impressions, while obscuring the movements, did not hinder their conversion into signs of recall or did not make it always more or less incomplete.

When the movements serve to recall or to manifest impressions with which they have coöperated, one can properly call them *first* or *natural signs;* but as soon as the individual has been caused to note these first functions, he extends them by an act of reflection founded upon the great law of the association of ideas, to many other sorts of being which have relations with these movements which are only more or less indirect and often even purely conventional. He thus transforms first signs into artificial or secondary ones and multiplies his means of correspondence either to the external world or with his own thought. He does more. He imparts to the most fleeting modifications a part of his surplus movements, forces them to enter into the sphere of his *memory* and creates after a fashion ends or motives for his will, where nothing of the kind existed.

Let us note, however, that these secondary functions have their limits fixed by the very nature of the organism. That which is not representable by these laws can hardly become so by any artifice and remain always in the number of more or less vague and confused memories. The artificial signs are only, if one may say so, grafted on natural signs.

In considering the signs from this point of view, it is plain how true it is to say that they are necessary for the formation of our *first ideas;* furthermore it is clearly plain that they are the only support of memory considered either in its origin or in its later development. It is plain in short that if a being were limited to *sensation,* he could have no signs, no ideas, no memory.

2. The imagination, we have said, could be considered as having more immediate relations with the *sensitivity* proper to the cerebral organ, and memory with its (the cerebral organ's) motor activity.[8] The products or the operations which depend

---

[8] Some scholars whom I honor and whose opinions are in some manner the awards that I look to, have not been fully satisfied with the distinction which I have established between memory and imagination. Their difficulties bear principally on the manner in which I express this distinction and on the physio-

on these two faculties seem to differ, in fact, as sensation differs from perception.

The recall of ideas, by their natural or artificial signs, leaves the individual all the calm necessary to contemplate them, to examine their details and apply his inner touch to them, so to speak, as he slowly applies his hand to a solid of which he wishes to know the form. The effort which accompanies recall has always an element of reflection and concentration in it, incompatible with very strong emotions and illusions of heightened sensitivity.

On the contrary, the spontaneous production of images, when it has a certain degree of vivacity, is always accompanied by affective feelings like—and often superior to—those which the presence of the object itself could excite; also the habitual exercise of the imagination heightens the sensory powers and reciprocally all that heightens these powers turns to the profit of the imagination.

But the activity of this faculty may be determined by different causes which, without changing its passive character, give to its products so many different degrees of energy and persistency, bring about so many differences in the way the images appear, that one would be tempted to relate them to really different faculties. It is necessary for us to show in a few words the chief among these causes.

---

logical ground that I suppose it to have. As that is an important point in my work, I must add some explanations.

1. The preceding analyses of the senses, I think, show that our different impressions can and ought really to be distinguished as *passive* and *active*, *sensitive* and *perceptive*; the latter depend more on the faculty of moving; the former more exclusively concern the faculty of feeling: *will* determines and directs the one; it is subordinate and negligible in the case of the other.

But what is said of impressions must necessarily be applied or extended to ideas; for the production of the idea (considered as a *copy*) is only, so to say, the replica of the antecedent operation of the senses. In order to imagine or recall, the organ of thought must resume a form and a modification like those which it had in perception itself. When, for example, I imagine the figure or form of an object, when I recall to myself a series of sounds, my brain is, doubtless, adjusted in the same manner (approximately) as if the eye or the hand actually ran over the dimensions of the solid or as if the ear was struck by

1. As soon as sight has intimately associated all its operations with the exercise of the motor faculty, it goes still farther, embraces vast perspectives simultaneously, and always, in spite of the will which directs it, groups about the principal object on which it is fixated, various secondary features by which it is surrounded. This association now becomes fixed and persists in the organ of thought; and the copy has the same arrangement as the original external image; if, therefore, one of the secondary features then chances to be reproduced to sight in isolation, it will cause the more or less lively imaginary appearance of the whole picture. Similarly, if the main object is reproduced alone, or surrounded by new secondary objects, it will revive the image of the concomitants first perceived, etc.

All this happens in the brain of the individual without his taking any active part in it. The play of his imagination is mingled and merged with that of external sense often without his being able to distinguish their products. He thinks that he simply sees, *senses*, and he imagines, compares, even acts as the result of many judgments of which he is not conscious at the time.

---

sonorous vibrations. Now, *perceptions* of forms and sounds could not take place without real and sensible movements, voluntarily executed in the organs, in the muscles of the hand and the eye, the ear and the voice; thus the production of corresponding *ideas* must also depend upon like determinations or upon an analogous *motor* reaction.

But they say to me, "The simple recall of our ideas and the secret exercise of our thinking faculty are not accompanied by any sensible movements: the cerebral center alone is then properly in activity; all happens within it. The muscular organ is in perfect repose; the supposition that you make movements executed in recall is, therefore, gratuitous or at least your language is inexact and presents a physiological error."

I answer first (to put a stop to every verbal difficulty) that I use the term *movement* in general to express any act of will, any employment of centrally initiated motor activity, whether this employment is apparent externally by the execution of muscular movements or is limited to a simple determination, which, having no external mark, is apparent only to the individual through consciousness of what I have called *effort*. Thus, in solitary meditation, in the midst of the most apparent repose and silence, I do not recognize, I do not feel the least movements of articulation which accompany or determine the

This mode of exercise of the imagination is allied to a host of habits of which we shall speak. We relate it principally to sight, because sight tends especially towards composition, towards associations by simultaneity, because in short, it is the principal instrument of synthesis. But the other senses also take more or less part in it in proportion to the "perceptuality" of their impressions. The objects themselves, whose presence determines the appearance of images or of the total picture with which they have been associated as elements, may be called *signs*. They have, in fact, with the *signs* of recall or movements (for which this qualification seems to me more fitting), the common, but unique, property of putting the individual again in a state like the one in which he already has been. But they fill this function of signs exclusively for the imagination; they are founded entirely on its passive character and merely extend its scope and re-enforce it.

2. Independently of all external stimulus, the cerebral center can initiate thought either by its own power and by virtue of acquired determinations or by abnormal causes which directly irritate its substance or finally by irradiations from internal organs, which, without being directly dependent on it for the accomplishment of their ordinary functions, are none the less bound to it by a sympathy about which a host of phenomena do not allow one to doubt.

---

regular recall of my ideas: is speech, on account of being internal, any the less a vocal movement? . . . . And when the blind man imagines and combines in his brain ideas of tactile forms, must not his hand respond and consent, if I may say so, to these representations? "Memory," as Condillac has said (see *La Logique*, Chapter IX) but in a different sense from mine," has its seat not only in the brain; it must also have it wherever there is the occasional cause of the ideas that we recall; now, if in order to give us the first time an idea (a perception) it was necessary for the senses to have acted on the brain (and, I add, for the brain to have acted to move the senses in a certain manner); it would seem that the memory of this idea will never be clearer than when the brain in its turn will act on the senses." (I say when the brain will react on the organs, in order to imprint on them movements like those which took place in perception.) It seems to me that the difficulty on this point is sufficiently clarified.

To these diverse causes are attached as many particular modes of the exercise of the imagination: the first, and without doubt the most frequent, is the one which has the most trifling results; they are perpetually confused with the activity of the senses as long as we are on the watch; and when the objects have disappeared, they replace them, follow one upon the other, push one another forward rapidly in the organ of thought, like surging waves. The two other causes are distinguished by the vivacity and energy of their results; they contribute equally to the different degrees of mania, madness, visions, ecstasies, dreams, astonishing effects of somnambulism, etc. All these modes are alike in that the individual's will takes no part in them and in that he is affected, pursued, drawn along in spite of himself by attractive images—be they sad or painful. The persistence, the obstinacy of these images, their particular tone, the force of the passions which are joined to them, the relations which they have with the satisfaction of natural needs or habit, the periodicity of their appearance, which concurs with the alternate sleep and awaking of the organs of the appetite, are so many indications which can enlighten us on the nature and the seat of their productive causes or at least (and this is what interests us here particularly) on the similarity, the close correspondence which binds the operations of *feeling* with those of *imagination*.

---

2. To the use of *motor activity* in voluntary recall in the exercise of *memory*, I have opposed the *sensory activity* of the cerebral center in the spontaneous reproduction of images or the passive exercise of *imagination*. This distinction appeared too hypothetical, at least in form: I shall no longer try to justify it entirely in this regard. When I borrowed terms from physiology to explain ideological facts, I did not intend to establish an absolute parallel between two orders of phenomena, which differ in many points, but only to indicate analogies which seemed to me fitting to throw some light on the principles of the science and which have been in general too little observed by metaphysicians. I pray, therefore, that the parallel be not pressed too closely. A master on whose authority I like to lean, distinguishes two sorts of reaction from the central nervous system, which concur (unequally in my opinion) in our different impressions, form them, and complete them: to these two modes of reaction (the one for *feeling*, the other for *movement*, which are exercised together and are now in equilibrium, now predominant, according as the individual

Let us end here the investigation and the long enumeration of the *data* of our subject. We have just seen how the exercise of memory and imagination is immediately derived from the very nature of impressions, or from the way in which the active and sensible being *perceives* or *feels* the action of objects; we shall see in the following how all operations, even those apparently furtherest removed from the senses, are equally referred to one or the other of these two sources; and the particular mode of influence which habit will exercise on these operations will serve to show us the faculty upon which they depend and the class in which we must rank them. Thus this whole memoir, if one may say so, will be only the continuation of the analyses above, and ought to serve at the same time to confirm them, if they are correct.

The outline of my work is already indicated in the way in which I have laid its foundations.

1. I shall first examine what is the influence of habit upon the faculty of sensing; or how the repetition of the same *sensations* (the same passive impressions) modifies this faculty.

2. What is the effect of the repetition of the same movements, considered as the natural and primary signs of the impressions which they help to produce and which they serve to distinguish, to fixate, to transform into *perceptions*.

---

perceives or *feels* the activity of the objects) must correspond two determinations of the same order, motor and sensory. The first prevails in the exercise of this active faculty of recall, which I have called memory; and the second in this passive faculty, which I call imagination. There is the ground of the hypothesis.

Now abandoning all explanation drawn from physiology, let us take only, if you wish, these terms of *sensory* and *motor* activity for two generic names (such as those of all causes) under which it is a question of ranking two classes of facts, which it is important not to confuse. These facts at least remain for us: they are certain, palpable, and every distinction which rests upon them will be sufficiently justified. Now, we recognize by experience and by observation of ourselves, that there are certain ideas which we recall voluntarily with a felt effort and some images which often arise in spite of us in the thinking organ, fill it, beset it, in some manner, without our having any more power to distract them than to evoke them; that these images correspond to the perceptions in which will, motor activity, less sensibly intervenes; that their

3. How these perceptions, formed and repeated in the same order, successive or simultaneous, being closely associated in the cerebral organ, become signs for the imagination and thus acquire a representative capacity far removed from their own individual character and cause a host of judgments, which are confused in the impression itself by their rapidity and ease.

The faculty of perceiving is associated directly with the imagination (considered simply as a representative function) and habit influences the operations of the senses only in making them concur with the exercise of the imagination. We shall, therefore, not separate these effects, but shall examine them in their reciprocal relations.

4. The imagination, considered as a modification of the sensitivity of the cerebral organ, is subject to different internal causes of excitation, which produce particular habits more or less persistent; whereupon depend in part the factitious passions which tyrannize over our kind. We shall try to recognize the principal effects of these habits.

We shall unite these four investigations in a first section, which will include what we shall call the *passive habits*. In fact, the majority of the operations of which we have just spoken arrange themselves in the class that we have thus

---

reproduction, their persistency, their tenacity always coincides with certain organic dispositions, with an heightening of sensibility, of nervous affections, sometimes deteriorations, either in the very substance of the brain or in other seats of sensibility, in some internal organs, the disposition of which, transformed into temperament, always impresses on the imagination a direction, a color, a particular tone.

Finally it is well recognized that man orders his *memory*, while he is led by his *imagination;* and who has not experienced these two states, often at the same time, when, being occupied in recalling an ordered series of signs and ideas, another simultaneous series of importunate phantoms comes to trouble and distract the regular activity of thought? It was, therefore, useful, even necessary, that language perpetuate this real distinction between two principal modifications of the thinking being, and that theory assign a reason for it.

Furthermore, as these principles have been established only in view of the question proposed, it is through it that they will receive the development and the degree of confirmation of which they are susceptible. I pray, therefore, that all judgment on their reality and their utility be suspended until their application is seen in the remainder of this work.

designated, while the others attain very promptly that degree
of facility in which the individual has absolutely no consciousness of the activity which he exercises in order to produce
them. Besides these operations, converted into habits, are
never anything but the product of the repetition of the same
external circumstances, acts, and movements which the individual has been caused, *forced* in some way, to execute by
himself or by the external world; if he were limited to these
habits, he would forever be ignorant of the power which he has
to modify himself, and his will, like his power, would be circumscribed within narrow limits by habit itself.

Real activity, taken in the ideological sense, therefore, begins
only with the use of signs voluntarily associated with the
impressions (or observed by the individual in these impressions
themselves) with the intention of communicating with others
or with his own thought. This faculty, peculiar to man, of
converting his movements or natural signs into artificial ones,
causes by its repeated exercise and the different modes of this
exercise, a class of habits which, while not differing essentially
from the first, are nevertheless transformed, in the unlimited
development of our perfectibility, in such a way as to appear
to obey special laws. After having established the foundation
of these habits, we shall examine in the second section (which
will have as its title *active habits*) their ideological effects, which
are allied principally to the exercise of *memory*, of which we
shall distinguish different kinds, following the nature of the
impressions or the ideas associated with the signs and the mode
itself of these associations. The recall of ideas by their signs
involves the judgments pronounced on the value of the latter
or on the relations of the ideas themselves. On the other hand,
our judgments follow each other in the habitual order which
memory gives to our signs. Hence the methods or forms of
reasoning which become for us *mechanical habits* in which we
allow ourselves to be carried along as in familiar sequences
of movements.

These different habits have many points of contact with

errors, inveterate prejudices of every kind, as well as with the enlightenment and the improvement of the human mind. We have not always been able to avoid insisting upon this important subject.

Restricted to the precise terms of the question, this memoir would have been shorter and, doubtless, better. But, in a subject which has relations to everything, I have often experienced how difficult it is to limit myself.

However imperfect my work still is, I have dared to reproduce it, not through a feeling of conceit, but as a testimony of the respect and obedience which I owe to the enlightened judges who did not disdain to encourage my first efforts.

FIRST SECTION

ON PASSIVE HABITS

> My mind has become a retreat,
> wherein I have tasted pleasures which
> have made me forget my afflictions.
> —BONNET, *Préface de l'Essai analy-*
> *tique de l'âme.*

CHAPTER I

The Influence of Habit upon Sensation

CONTINUED AND REPEATED SENSATIONS

All our impressions, of whatever nature they be, grow gradually weaker when they are continued for a certain time or frequently repeated. There is no exception, save for cases where the cause of the impression goes to the point of injuring or destroying the organ.

This observation is very general and very common. It is confirmed by our experience every day and every instant. Nevertheless, it includes a particular circumstance which does not appear to have been sufficiently noticed, although it is equally easy to perceive; that is, that among these repeated impressions which are continually growing weaker, some become more and more obscured and tend to vanish entirely, whereas others—while arousing less interest—not only retain all their clearness, but often even acquire greater distinctness. This fact alone, which is beyond all argument, would suffice, doubtless, to disclose an essential difference of character between sensations which degenerate and fade out and perceptions which become clear, even if we did not know this difference for other reasons.

If I am for a long time exposed to the same degree of temperature, if I frequently sense the same odor or the same taste, I will end by sensing nothing at all, and although the external cause in both cases continues to subsist, it will be for me as if it did not exist.

Resistance, degrees of light, colors, sounds grow weaker also through repetition or continuance, but it often happens that the less we *feel*, the more we *perceive*. These two classes of impressions, therefore, cannot be related to one and the same faculty; for it would be necessary to suppose that this single faculty could become all at once more inert and more active through the same influence of habit. Let us first examine how the sensation becomes deadened and paralysed and what are the principal circumstances which accompany this process of decay. We shall then study its opposite in the increasing improvement of our perceptive faculty.

CONJECTURES ON THE MANNER IN WHICH CONTINUED OR REPEATED SENSATIONS GROW WEAKER

I. The phenomenon of the weakening of sensations when repeated is as simple as these sensations themselves. We have no need to seek its causes in judgments or in comparisons of one perceived condition and another, since we have seen that these are foreign to these modifications considered in isolation. The immediate and sole cause here very evidently lies in the activity of the organs, which varies successively under equal and repeated stimulation by the same objects; but this cause, separated from all extraneous properties and reduced to its state of simplicity, is only the more difficult to know. In order to know how a continued sensation grows weaker, we should need to know how it begins, for it is always the result of the same activity, of the same organic condition. But this initial activity, this primary condition, is concealed from our eyes, like all first causes, by an impenetrable veil. Nevertheless, let us make an hypothesis, not in order to discover the secret of nature, but in order to elucidate the facts and find their interrelations.

The principle of life, in whatever way one considers it, sustains ceaselessly, in the organic whole that it animates, and in each part of this whole, various internal movements which are not at all open to direct observation, are insensible to the individual in his natural state and do not enter into the sphere of his *activity*, in the strict sense of the term.

The degree or intensity of vital movement engaged in by each part or organ is proportional on the one hand to the basic forces which the life principle has at its command, and on the other hand to the particular rôle which this organ must play, the functions which it must perform in the system to which it is closely bound.   That is what constitutes what I shall call the *natural tone*, the sensitivity proper to each and every one of its parts.

The system may be said to be in equilibrium when the vital forces are equally or proportionately divided and when each organ remains in its natural tone or in a tone relative to that of the others.   In this state the individual has only a uniform feeling of existence, and if one should suppose that all was in repose around him and should abstract from all external *mobility*, this inalienable feeling which is inseparable from life itself would subsist no less, although it would, doubtless, be more obscure than anything that we can imagine from our experience.

But the tone of the organs is susceptible of variátion, and varies in fact necessarily with the action of all the internal and external causes which can either increase simultaneously the forces of the system as a whole, or bring about some change in the relative state of a part.   In this latter case, the life, the feeling which is proper to this part, again emerges, so to say, from the general life in which it had been merged.   The animal experiences a *sensation* which is proportional to the magnitude of the change and persists until an equilibrium is again established.

Now, the sensitive principle (which ought to be considered an essentially active force) always has a tendency to restore this equilibrium, either by lowering the tone of the stimulated organ or by successively raising that of the whole until the original ratio between them is re-established.

The more this ratio is disturbed, the greater is the change and the more vivid is the sensation.   Hence it follows that the first instant when an exciting cause acts on an organ and raises its tone, is also the one when its effect is most energetic.   In proportion as the equilibrium is re-established, i.e., in proportion as the ratio tends to become restored, the sensation diminishes, as by a succession of oscillations decreasing in amplitude, until it dissolves again, so to speak, in the uniform feeling of existence.

In the second place, the intensity of the activity of the *object* (or of whatever causes the impression) is relative to the change caused in the tone of the part upon which it acts; but the object acts only by the quantity of its movement and this movement has a certain relation with that which constitutes the tone of the organ. It may tend to accelerate or to diminish it in several ways, to be opposed to it or to coöperate with it and leave it almost in the same state; hence there is an infinity of modes in sensation.

If the movement of the object is too much opposed to that of the organ, or predominates over it to a certain point, the sensation is more or less painful, and in this case either the sensitive principle makes vain efforts to restore the equilibrium and struggle against the cause and the pain persists and increases, or else the ratio of the forces is re-established only by slow degrees, and the individual gradually suffers less until he feels nothing more—until he is, as we say, *accustomed to the pain*.

If the movement of the object concurs with the tone of the organ and merely increases it up to a certain point, the sensation is agreeable in the first moments, but it tends to disappear much more promptly. It seems, in fact, that whatever be the change in the organic state which constitutes pleasure, it is very little removed from the natural state—the state characteristic of the parts which are its seat. For one degree more produces pain, one degree less, indifference, and its continuance soon causes it to disappear altogether—which shows clearly the delicacy of our purely sensuous enjoyments.

If we start from the change of tone which corresponds to pain and follow all the successive degrees of diminution which lead to insensibility, we may pass through the zone of pleasure.

This is a compensation contrived by nature for the being who has more suffering than enjoyment.

But, whatever be the cause which tends to change the state of an organ or of the system, it is plain that the intensity of its emotional effect depends at the outset on its relation to the tone of the organ at that time. Now, this tone varies continually through the determinations of the life principle alone. Therefore, regarding only the instantaneous effect of the same cause and supposing it to be reproduced at sufficiently long intervals, its modes of action may be different or even absolutely opposed, according to the changes in the conditions of sensitivity. If it is equally and constantly applied, these conditions, varying incessantly in order to resume their state of equilibrium, continually weaken its effect, however intense it had been at first (aside from the case of sudden lesion), and will end by making it insensible. If one supposed that the cause—always constant—instead of remaining the same varied slowly and by degrees from the mode which most approximates the original tone of the organ to one which is furtherest removed from it, each change being slight in itself, no affective modification would result but a simple succession of organic states, a successive elevation of all the forces, which would always keep the same relation between them. It is thus that every affection, every deterioration which takes place gradually in the organs—even those essential to the maintenance of life—occasions in the individual no particular feeling, but is transformed into *temperament* by its very duration. Thus it is that habit hides from us the troubles and disorders of our functions when they are slowly upset, that we pass without our perceiving it through successive modifications corresponding to the ages, temperaments, kinds of life, climates, etc., that everything in us is in a perpetual flux, while we think we are always the same; that we die at every instant, while we wish to be immortal. It is thus, in short, that our nature becomes so flexible, the modes of our vitality so extended, and that the same cause which makes pleasures so fleeting also makes pain less violent and existence more assured.

It follows from all that precedes; first, that the diminishing of our continued sensations does not depend on mechanical causes (that is to say *material* causes) such as one could imagine of several kinds, but rather that it is a result of the *activity* of the very principle which produces these sensations;[1] second, that the effects and the circumstances of this gradual weakening concur to prove the existence and the real activity of this principle inherent in organic and sensitive bodies; third, that there is no necessary relation between the manner of acting of any external cause and its sensory product, since—the cause remaining the same—the product passes through all differences of degradation to complete fading away; fourth, that this last effect probably takes place only in as far as the sensory forces, first more poignantly stimulated and in some way accumulated in an organ by the continual application of the provoking cause are successively restored to the same equilibrium in which they were before the impression, as electric fluid, accumulated in a closed system, is manifest only when it is unequally distributed, and remains inactive or invisible when its equilibrium is re-established.

All that we have said of continued sensations applies in the same way to repeated sensations. After a stimulus has acted long enough and with sufficient force on an organ it changes the state of the organ by raising, at the outset, its relative tone; but, on the other hand, the sensitive principle raises the forces of the system, in order to put them, so to speak, on a level with this stimulation and maintain the same ratio as before. The organ remains for a certain time in this condition. If, while that condition persists, the same cause chances to act again, it is evident that it must produce less change than at first, since it finds the organ and the system already partly pitched to the tone to which it tends to bring them, and since it consequently changes the ratio of the forces much less. The

---

[1] It is well known that it is necessary to distinguish this *sensory activity* (which phenomena force us to admit, but which is exercised in us unconsciously) from motor activity or *voluntary determinations*.

sensation will, therefore, be less intense. The more frequent the repetitions are and the more rapidly they succeed each other, the more the effect will approximate continuity. If the intervals were sufficiently long for the system and the organ to be restored to their primitive state, it is obvious that the repeated sensation would have the same effect as a new one.

The preceding hypothesis can in general apply to every impression, every stimulation continued or repeated in any organ; but all organs do not admit of equally continuous impressions nor of equally vivid stimulations. The more passive, the more devoid of mobility they are—the more feeling predominates over movement in them, the more also (and because of their very formation) are they helpless before the cause which irritates them and which may continue to act upon them—the more, in short, the sensory effect is isolated and accomplished without disturbance. On the other hand, these same passive organs have more extended sympathies, closer relations with the special centers of feeling. They are themselves sometimes seats of it. Stimulating them, therefore, affects the whole system and can modify its powers and determine its general activity. It will be, therefore, to impressions of this kind that our hypothesis will be more directly applicable. If we are limited to a consideration of these impressions in their primary aspect, as *passive*, our hypothesis will explain very well the circumstances of their deterioration by habit. In their secondary aspect, as *active*, the same hypothesis will afford the clue to various other phenomena which coöperate in the weakening of sensations and which at first appear to be opposed to the ordinary effects of habit, as the increase of needs and the violence of desires on the one hand, corresponding to indifference on the other, to the periodicity of these needs and in certain cases the invariability of the same sensations no matter how frequently they are repeated. These phenomena evidently cannot be reconciled with the mechanical hypotheses *of an increase of mobility* or *of an artificial callousness of the parts*, hypotheses which are often used to explain the weakening of repeated impressions.

Let us successively examine the effects of habit in these two aspects, that is to say, on impressions considered as *passive* and as *active*.

THE IMPRESSIONS MOST WEAKENED BY REPETITION

II. Our sensations certainly fade and vanish sooner and more completely in proportion to the *passivity* of their respective organs. This condition is bound up with the forced continuance of impressions, since then the will cannot directly react to distract or to stop them.

And first, inner impressions, however little they persist in the same degree, tend to be converted into habits of *temperament* and, although in this state they continue to influence the feeling of existence, which they make sad or painful, easy or agreeable, they cease nevertheless to be felt in themselves, but are lost and merged in this multitude of vague impressions, which coöperate to form the habitual inner feeling of our passive existence. Such an effect indeed seems to be connected with the equilibrium or the equal reaction of sensory forces which are coördinated with each other in course of time in such a way that one impression does not continue to dominate too much over the others. But we shall consider them soon in another connection.

Passive touch, spread over the whole surface of the body, is exposed at all points to the equal, continued or varied excitation of surrounding fluids or objects in motion, which stimulate it, titillate it, prick it, etc., without its being able to react in order to change or suspend their effects. But sensitivity is incessantly on the watch and puts itself on an equality with impressions by moderating and annulling them (always excepting cases of serious and sudden lesions).

The equilibrium of which we have spoken and the action of the sensory principle to re-establish it, are manifest in no other kind of impressions more clearly than in those which correspond to tactile sensations and particularly to those of heat or cold. It is well known how easily our bodies are adapted to changes of climate and temperature,[2] provided that the transition is not too sudden; how a uniform temperature long continued becomes insensible to us; how the sensation is always proportional to the actual condition of the organ (so that such and such a degree alternately freezes or burns us); how from this organ it is extended from point to point and affects us the more intensely the more concentrated it is. In short, it is well known that the sensitive principle always tends to maintain in us an almost even heat, which it can do only by successively raising or lowering our temperature and restoring the inner equilibrium, which without this activity would be disturbed every instant.

Odors also gradually become fainter and end by becoming insensible. "My sachet scented with flowers," said Montaigne, "is first of service to my nose; but, after I have used it a week, it is no longer of any use except to the noses of bystanders." Odors are necessarily continuous since their organ is passive and breathing cannot be interrupted. First they stimulate the whole system, which atunes itself to them and soon ceases to experience any change from them. In relation to appetite they have other effects which we shall presently indicate.

Tastes become deadened more through repetition than through their continuance and always in proportion as the organ is more passive in experiencing them. Many an agreeable or disagreeable taste, which has affected us in the beginning, particularly in a drink, soon becomes through custom absolutely insensible—nauseous flavors excepted. Taste, like odor, becomes accustomed to the strongest artificial irritants and it is almost paralysed by their repeated activity and, nevertheless, these same irritants become imperious needs.

[2] "Habit can give man the power of conserving the heat which is characteristic of him, when he passes *suddenly* through opposite and extreme conditions of atmospheric temperature." (See Barthez, *Nouveaux éléments de la science de l'homme.*)

Sounds, considered as passive impressions of an organ devoid of mobility, can undergo all the gradual fading which results from the repetition and continuance to which they are particularly susceptible. We experience daily how easy it is to become accustomed to every kind of noise to the point of becoming absolutely unconscious of it. This body, this *material* of sound, moreover, which in the beginning affects us so poignantly by itself and independently of any perceived relation, of any effect of melody, loses also through its frequency all power to stimulate. But though the impression in this case weakens like sensation, it is not obedient to the same law, to the same mode of diminishing, as perception. The motor activity, combined with the sensory, changes the simple results and gives rise to other habits. The auditory impression may lose its power of attraction, but the vocal impression will keep its distinctness.

Light first stimulates the fibres of the retina with a certain force. Sensitivity—put into play—contracts or dilates the pupil through an activity quite independent of the will. It raises the tone of the organ, adjusts it, accommodates it to the degree of the external stimulus, in such a way that it is no longer affected, that it no longer feels the continued or repeated impression in the same degree.

If the eye were motionless, if its impressions were isolated, would not habit weaken colors as it does odors, flavors, etc.? It is probable that the effect would not be the same; for the functions of the center, to which colors seem to be particularly suited, differ from purely sensory functions.

Be that as it may, since the voluntary action of the different muscles of the eye always coincides with the nervous excitation of the retina, since the organ itself is animated by its own movements,—amplifies the action of luminous rays when they are too feeble, moderates them or avoids them when they might be injurious to it—the action of the sensory forces will even here meet with powerful distractions; the results of habit will be divided between diminution on the one hand and persistence or intensification on the other.

These observations, it seems to me, prove that habit weakens our impressions only in proportion to their passivity; that the intervention of motor activity is sufficient to make this result vary by introducing other effects, which are not subject to the same law nor to the same modes of degradation and to which the preceding hypothesis cannot be applicable.

Let us now examine our continuous or repeated sensations in relation to active impressions.

WHY IT IS NECESSARY TO REPEAT ACTIVE IMPRESSIONS AS THEY GROW WEAK

III. To every active impression of feeling correspond two effects which we have already distinguished, namely, the change made in the tone of the organ and the progressive heightening of the forces of the system, which tend to put themselves, if one may say so, on the same level. This last effect must be so much the more necessary and more marked as the stimulated organ has more extended communications or sympathies and as the excitation, at first more lively, has been more continuous or more often repeated; then, in proportion as the sensation gets fainter and deteriorates in the organ (which is perhaps already beginning to become callous), the system, or the center most directly interested, does not remain less fixed at the same tone and the sensory principle always keeps some more or less persistent determination of it; it will, therefore, still act when the exciting cause happens to be lacking. In proportion as the tone of the organ is lowered, it will make a kind of effort to raise it and restore to it the activity that it had received from it. The fruitlessness of this effort will produce trouble, discomfort, uneasiness, *desire*. If during this time of inner agitation, the same cause chances to be renewed, there will be an instant of calm. But sensitivity will not be at its maximum, since its determinations are always in excess of the real affective product and since the impression, becoming gradually weaker and weaker through repetition, succeeds only in exciting the need without being able to satisfy it. Thus it is that the being who is accustomed to artificial excitement, is indifferent to pleasure when he has it, yet feels himself cruelly tormented by the loss of it.

If the cause had repeated its action several times in equal and measured intervals, the center interested would not fail to become animated at the time, at the hour fixed by habit. There would be a new action on the organ to raise its tone, and therefore, new discomfort, new desires. Doubtless, nothing proves better the peculiar action of the inner source of our sensations than this spontaneous alternating and periodical awakening and sleep of the sensible centers. But also nothing seems to show more clearly to me a real difference between the principle of instinct and appetite and that of reasoned determinations founded upon experience; between vague wishes and the *will* which aims at a goal, between needs and faculties. Doubtless, they are intimately related and correspond to each other more closely as life progresses, but ought none the less to be distinguished according to the difference of origin and the contrary results which the influence itself of habit discloses to us.

Besides acquired determinations corresponding to repeated artificial excitations, phenomena further indicate in internal organs, or sense centers, natural determinations which are really instinctive and prior to the exercise of the senses. These determinations being executed spontaneously, following the primordial laws of vitality, remain independent, up to a certain point, of the sway of habit. They are especially distinguished in that they resist its deteriorating influence and keep for the simple impressions, which are suited to them, an ever fresh attraction, which the most frequent repetition cannot cause to fade. Thus the stomach desires foods which suit it, is attracted to them to a certain extent and impels towards them the sensitive and active being whose will has not yet had time to be born. In vain the impressions of these foods excite the organs of taste and smell frequently. As long as they correspond to nature's needs, they remain incorruptible. A constant inner force incessantly rejuvenates these organs and prevents them from being blunted. Bread and water have always the same relish for one who awaits the impulsion of need, whereas artificial, capricious desires are stimulated and blunted through habit. This last cause acts, therefore, to diminish impressions only in so far as it alone has determined the necessity for them and it is through this notable circumstance that we can recognize its results.

The senses particularly related to appetite are, therefore, not susceptible as the others of being perfected by exercise. Their mode of cultivation is in a manner abstinence. They are always sufficiently strong and acute, so long as they are influenced by natural activity and are not yet perverted from the sensory centers with which they are in relation. See what sensitiveness smell assumes suddenly at the very time when the sixth sense develops! They appear to emerge together from their torpor. See this starving savage discover the game and follow its track.

It is repeated artificial stimulations which blunt our sense organs, pervert their instinct, submit all our functions, all our needs to the sway of habit, and thus progressively extend its dulling power over all our pleasures.

Doubtless, this is enough and perhaps too much on a subject which appears in many points to be far from the principal object of our research. But we needed to determine clearly the influence of habit on the immediate products of sensibility and to recognize, through the mode of this influence, through the degradation and transiency of its results, that it is not with this source that the progress of our perfectible faculties is connected.

CHAPTER II

INFLUENCE OF HABIT UPON PERCEPTION

REPEATED PERCEPTIONS; HOW THEY BECOME MORE DISTINCT

If all the faculties of man were reduced to sensation and to its different modes, habit would exercise on them the most sinister influence. Aside from natural needs and in all the intervals which would separate their periodic attacks, the sensitive being, no longer receiving from his accustomed impressions, this stimulating activity which is life, would remain sunk in a state of sleep or torpor. All exercise would become for him a debilitating principle and, if one may say so, a principle of death. In the midst of ever variable modifications, which would flee far from him and disappear without return, where would be, I do not say the opportunities and means of perfectibility, but even the common chain which would unite the different periods, the different instants of passive existence?

When on the one hand we reflect on the instability of all our affective modifications, on the promptitude with which they escape us, on how the progress of age can blunt our sensibility and render it partly callous; and when on the other hand we consider the gradual extension of the reach of our active senses (alone susceptible of true education), the power, the skill the increasing agility of our motor organs, the rapid perfecting of the faculties which are most directly related to their exercise, the multitude of judgments and complicated operations which enter into this exercise—now apparently so simple —could we mistake the real origin of all our progress and not see that it is with our motor faculties that the most useful and most fortunate influence of habit is primarily connected?

It is to habit that we owe the facility, the precision, and the extreme rapidity of all our motions and voluntary operations;

100

but it is habit also which hides from us their nature and quantity. "It hides from us the part that it plays precisely because it dominates to the highest degree." Let us try to force from it a part of its secret and to unravel some of the elements of these complex results. Let us see first how the faculty of perceiving is extended and perfected by the continual repetition of its exercise.

Three causes or principal circumstances coöperate to make a repeated impression more distinct and to adapt it to the perceptive faculty: first, diminution of the original sensory effect; second, increasing facility and differentiation of the motions proper, on which its active character depends; third, association with other motions which it determines or with other impressions which coincide with it and serve as so many signs and characteristic marks to distinguish it and to enable it to be recognized when it is repeated. We shall successively examine each of these circumstances.

THE DIMINUTION OF REPEATED SENSATION—THE FIRST CAUSE
OF DIFFERENTIATION

I. What we have said of passive impressions in the Introduction of this Memoir and of repeated sensations in the preceding chapter, exempts us from entering into lengthy details on this first effect of habit.

There cannot be distinct vision, if the activity of light is too strong, considering the sensibility and the actual tone of the organ; or even if too vivid, too brilliant colors strike and dazzle the sight and distract it from the forms and contours which delineate their shades. There would hardly be an effect of harmony, if all the *timbres* of instruments were of such a nature as to produce on the ear and on the sensory system the effect of the harmonica or of a bell. Finally there would not be distinct perception of tangible forms, if the hand were continually titillated or pricked, fretted by the satin-like smoothness or the roughness of surfaces. Whatever were the mode of external activity, the function of perceiving would remain equally

null and without exercise, if sight were naturally as delicate as
it is in ophthalmia, if hearing had the susceptibility which is
observed in certain nervous affections and if the skin of the
hand was as sensitive as that which covers the penis or the
lips.

Such is the state of the child at the beginning of its existence.
Everything startles, irritates, hurts it; it has *felt* long before
it perceives.

By repeated activity of the same objects and the necessary
course of life, all the external organs become hardened. The
sensitive being is put on a footing with the causes of irritation
which rule him, struggles against them successfully, moderates,
weakens or even reduces their impressions to nothing. All
that which impresses only by its purely affective qualities
loses its influence. The circle of sensations shrinks, the field
of perceptions opens and spreads; motor activities develop; the
individual no longer passively awaits the action of objects
upon him; he goes out to them, converts them to his use, disposes of them as of materials obedient to his power.

When habit weakens impressions it begins to bring them together, to put them in some degree within reach of the perceptive faculty, but its influence, considered from this first point
of view, is still only passive, conditional, setting the stage rather
than playing the drama.[1] Its function consists only in clear-
ing away obstacles and preparing the way for perception. But
the latter cannot really be brought to pass and assume its
active character except by the intervention and direct exercise
of mobility. It is here that all increasing progress, of which
habit is the motive power, begins.

FACILITY AND PRECISION OF MOVEMENTS IN THE ORGANS—
SECOND CAUSE.

II. Although the successive advances of the primary education of our senses or original faculties, have not perhaps been
observed as carefully as their importance would demand;

---

[1] This terminal clause is my paraphrase for the French *prédisposant.*—TR.

although observation here is so much the more delicate or difficult because it cannot be aided, much less supplemented, by any introspection (*retour réfléchi sur notre expérience*), one can, however, hardly doubt that this education of the organs, which are customarily considered only sensory, begins by the development of their own or associated mobility and that it is in this progressive development that the influence of habit makes itself particularly felt.

Children first learn slowly enough to distinguish a few objects by sight. The organism must have acquired the degree of necessary steadiness to be able to fixate and it must then perform the different movements which distinct vision necessitates. But, this period coincides with that when touch itself begins to have enough power and skill to grasp objects and run over their surfaces. And surely there are no nice perceptions at different distances nor judgments of distances until after the child himself has walked or frequently been carried towards the different objects.

It appears indeed also that hearing, first struck by noise, is unable to distinguish sounds until the vocal instrument, the development of which is more tardy, has become capable of responding to it and reëchoing its impressions. The sensory organs thus first put the motor organs into play, but the latter react in their turn and, becoming perfected by repeated exercise, soon return to the others with interest what they have received from them.

In order to appreciate the mode and the results of this last progress, let us observe two principal, infallible, and always inseparable effects, which habit generally produces upon our motor faculty in whatever manner it is exercised. First, every voluntary movement frequently repeated becomes more and more easy, prompt, and precise. Second, effort or the resulting impression of movement grows weaker in the same proportion as the rapidity, precision, and facility increase and, in the last stage of this increase, movement, become quite insensible in itself, manifests itself no longer to consciousness except by the results with whose production it coöperates or the impressions with which it is associated.

These two general and constant principles, being applied in the same absolute manner to the simultaneous development of simple mobility and of the perceptive faculty, show first very clearly the analogy or rather the identity of the origin of these faculties.

They explain to us in the second place how the reaction, exercised by the center on an external motor sense, becoming ever prompter, easier (and consequently accompanied by a slighter perception or feeling of effort) in proportion as the activity of this organ is perfected, the perception may become more distinct and more precise on the one hand, while on the other the individual is more completely blinded to the active part which he takes in it, to the operations and judgments which join in giving it its form and character; in short, how the composite function of perception, tends always to approach, in promptitude, ease, and apparent passivity, *sensation* properly so-called.

It is thus, therefore, and by cloaking our motor activity in the extreme facility of its products, that habit effaces the line of demarcation between voluntary and involuntary acts, between acquisitions of experience and instinctive operations, between the faculty of feeling and that of perceiving; and when we then wish to lay bare the differences which separate these faculties, habit, which tends ever more vigorously to confuse them, shows them to us indivisibly united down to their cradle.

Yet let us pursue the thread of our analyses and, starting from these obscure points remote from all memories to which we have been wishing to attach it, let us first briefly indicate (since we have no details) the first influence which mobility acquired by the organs themselves can have on the distinct impressions which they transmit to us. We shall then better appreciate what the determinations and associations, formed in a common center, add to these impressions simultaneously or successively repeated, in order to complete them, clarify them, combine them, in short, correct some by means of others.

The will or—to substitute the effect (*le fait*) for the cause—
the reaction of the center first works directly upon the motor
organs as those work secondarily upon the objects; the organ
first resists the will, the objects resist the organ. By the first
resistance the active being knows the parts of his body; by
the second, he learns to know external objects; but habit must
have already made the one sufficiently familiar and almost imperceptible to the individual in order to be able to draw from
the other any exact and detailed information.

Before touch, for example, has acquired by exercise a certain
degree of power and mobility, its organs obey the will only with
difficulty; a conscious effort is necessary to teach them to
bend and adjust themselves to objects; this effort concentrates
the attention and distracts it from different kinds of external
resistance; the successive impressions, which unite necessarily
in a complex perception of *form*, are not yet sufficiently un-
raveled from each other, or follow each other with too much
confusion and slowness, to be able to be combined or distinguished.   In this first apprenticeship, the child is, therefore,
instructed to know and to direct his own organs rather than
to grasp and nicely circumscribe the extended object to which
he applies them; it is thus that the beginner in music, completely occupied with moving and placing his fingers and his
bow, hardly distinguishes the sounds that he draws from the
instrument.   The movements of the touch organ becoming
extremely easy through repetition, the muscular effort disappears or is no longer *felt* except in its product, *external resistance*.   Therefore, it is this which will henceforth attract his
whole attention.   Soon the individual, mistaking his own
activity, will transfer it entirely to the object, or *resistant term*,
will attribute to it the absolute qualities of inertia, solidity,
weight.   He will even be induced, furthermore, to consider
resistance as subsisting outside of him by itself, as he finds it
always invariable in the midst of all the other fleeting modifications which he attributes to himself and of which he feels himself to be the subject.

In fact, if we *felt* resistance as we feel many tactile qualities, there would be no impression which would be less *perceived*, since there is none more continuous. As long as we watch, it does not cease being present to us an instant; it interposes itself among all our states of being and even makes an essential part of the actual feeling that we have of our existence; but if its continuousness renders it very familiar and most frequently distracts us from it, the least return of attention gives back to it all its clearness and invariably shows it to us in the same manner.

The preceding observations likewise apply to the exercise of sight. Undoubtedly, it is principally because of the absence of habits of movement proper to the organ that those born blind, for some time after having undergone the operation for cataract, cannot yet see except very confusedly; they must make a certain effort, which demands all their application and occupies them, when they wish to turn or move their eyes, until the muscles have acquired all their mobility. Then perception is distinct, visual activity is executed perfectly, but the individual has no longer any consciousness of his activity (already instructed by touch) he transfers entirely its products to the external world. He perceives *naturally* and *without effort* the colored *figure* in the tactile *form*.

I do not know whether there is also a particular impression of effort corresponding to the movements of the small bones and muscles of the ear in a man who hears for the first time. What is certain is that the organ must be active in order to proportion the degrees of tension of the tympanic membrane to the force of the sounds and that it must have acquired enough mobility and precision in its activity to be able to distinguish or follow rapid articulations of voice, which is always the work of quite prolonged habit. But, when this habit is contracted, we distinguish vocal sounds of every kind, we execute complicated movements which their emission exacts with a facility and promptitude which frequently hides our own activity from us and always hinders us from perceiving its details.

As to the movements of smell and taste, they are learned naturally and determined instinctively. Their mechanism is almost as perfect in the beginning as after very prolonged experience, and that, added to all that we have said elsewhere, well proves that impressions of these senses have not such direct relations with the faculty of perceiving, the successive advances of which are so many acquisitions dependent on the perfected motility of the organs which are appropriate to it.

ASSOCIATION OF MOVEMENTS AND IMPRESSIONS IN A COMMON CENTER—THIRD CAUSE

III. If each impression always kept its proper and individual character or if it only introduced in the perception of the object operations directly connected with the present activity of the external sense to which this object is appropriate, one could perhaps conceive through what precedes, how habit influences these primary operations either in concealing them themselves through their facility or in giving to their products greater precision and clarity. But, when one wishes to examine a little more thoroughly what happens in our apparently simplest perceptions, when one considers that there is not one which is not a combined result of many others; that the individual, always comprehending more than his senses show him, now subsumes in one simultaneous act their successive impressions, now foresees them and is affected by them in advance; in short, that he does not separate his memories and impressions and perceives only in comparing; one then feels the necessity of reascending from the partial activity of the organs and the habits characteristic of each of them to the single center which receives, combines, transforms, interchanges their repeated products and which finally reacting with the sum of these acquired determinations, on any one of these simple products, powerfully modifies its original form, completes it, corrects it, alters its nature, ever unites with it some accessories which are foreign to it. One feels, in a word, that the habits of the imagination must concur with those of the senses, that they ceaselessly reappear in each other and that one cannot isolate their results. Let us now occupy ourselves, therefore, with this simultaneous co-operation, which has such a marked influence upon the progress and extension of our perceptive faculty.

First, let us imagine a blind man, applying his hand, already accustomed to exercise, to a new solid which has a certain number of angles and surfaces. It is certain that this blind man at first cannot embrace or simultaneously perceive more parts than his hand covers, and that the solid, however little extended it is and however simple its form, would be gone over and known only by successive movements. Now habit can indeed render these movements more prompt and precise, but how will it succeed in changing the manner of procedure in the organ and transforming succession into simultaneity? On the other hand, how could such a blind man as the geometer Saunderson have demonstrated *synthetically* the numerous properties of different geometric bodies, if, while he successively touched each of the surfaces of a solid, his thought had not simultaneously embraced their symmetrical order, or if the parts had not been developed and arranged in his brain in a sort of *tangible* perspective?

In order that the impressions, which succeed each other and which are external to each other, as are those of touch, could be combined and compared, it is necessary that the terms which compose this series of impressions be so brought together (without, nevertheless, being confused) that the trace or the idea of the first term still persists in all its force when the last is reached. But the present impression and the place of the one which has passed cannot persist together in sense, for one would eclipse the other and there would not be any comparison of association possible between the terms. It is, therefore, the internal and central organ which gathering one by one the successive products of external activity, alone can fix and keep them and subsume, so to speak, in one and the same framework, the impressions which now are striking the senses and those which have just escaped it in its course.

This being granted, one conceives how habit can facilitate in two ways for a blind man the distinct and almost simultaneous perception of the tangible compound. For, at first, the movements of touch becoming more precise, more detailed, and more rapid, the individual and successive impressions of resistance and of its modes will be better circumscribed and especially more closely connected, more firmly bound together in the chain which must unite them. In the second place, the corresponding active determinations of the central organ, acquiring through repetition more depth and power, will tend to be executed concurrently with the sense impressions with a greater promptitude and facility. But from then on perception will be almost entirely internal and the blind man will touch more, if I may say so, with his brain than with his hand. It will suffice for the external sense to give the first warning; the slightest contact and the simplest apprehension of the familiar object will put into play the imagination, already disposed to react, and the completed picture, the solid perspective, will instantly and without effort be unrolled. But we are going to see some more sensible examples of this influence of the imagination strengthened by habit upon our perceptive faculty.

Second, if the phenomena which are most closely connected and which a constant repetition has rendered very familiar to us, could yet surprise us, would it not really be astonishing that an organ as foreign as the eye to the impression of resistance, had succeeded in *guessing*, if one may say so, all forms and all appearances to the extent of making it doubtful whether nature has not directly suited it to this impression? An association so close, an adherence so unsurmountable between two sorts of heterogeneous impressions, testifies well to what habit can do to change the proper individual character of our sense impressions, to compound them, to combine some with others while keeping for the total product the appearance of a perfect simplicity.

The organs of touch and sight are essentially connected with each other through natural relations of motility and it is on this that the perfect coincidence and reciprocal transformation of their impressions especially depend. From the primary and uninterrupted co-operation of the two perceptions, visual and tactile, results a third which contains both, but which is neither one nor the other by itself. For certainly (whatever idea one can have in other respects of the characteristic functions of sight) we do not see as if we were not accustomed to touch and we do not touch as if we had never seen.

When the eye, trusting to its first habits, to the lessons that it has received from touch, begins to fly on its own wings and apprehends the color at the end of the rays where the hand had already met with resistance, this simple and isolated impression of color is sufficient to cause in the cerebral center the determination or the idea of resistance, associated by constant repetition. When the products of the inner organ thus mingle and become confused with those of the external sense, the individual who sees without touching finds himself in the same state as when he both saw and touched simultaneously. It is through the same effect that the simple contact with a surface represented to the blind man cited above the whole form of the familiar solid.

As sight alone grows to apprehend resistance in color, the hand in its turn grows to include color in resistance. The two impressions thus serve for reciprocal signs, and, confused by habit in an indivisible perception, are forever inseparable. The firmness of this bond, formed or prepared in part by nature, must perhaps surprise us less when we see quite artificial associations, cemented by habit alone, on the point of becoming almost as indissoluble.

Sight receives the more tardy completion of its education through the repeated and varied exercise of the faculty of locomotion. It is then that it reaches distances where touch cannot follow it, to confirm and correct its too frequently overhasty reports. The determinations of touch become more obscure in proportion as those of sight take more predominance.

The eye seems to have for its characteristic and exclusive function to measure space, to allot distances and to determine forms. Every modulation is in color, in the degree of shade or of light. Judgment has lost its natural basis. There is no longer a fixed relation. All is active, mobile, like the organ which seems to have usurped the whole domain of our perceptions. One habit replaces another and often destroys its effect; the individual accustomed, for example, to estimate the size of an object by its distance and distance by the intensity of the light rays or the number of intervening objects, will now follow habit, in spite of evidently contrary experience, now experience, in spite of the habit which ought to be opposed to it. If the image of a familiar object is strongly impressed on the mind, whatever be the visible appearances which correspond to its position, to its distance, to the lowering of the tints with which it is colored, the imagination will restore to it its forms, its dimensions, almost all its former clearness and will then react to modify the external sense, as the latter had acted previously in order to strengthen it. The slightest warning and the remotest attendant circumstances will suffice to determine this inner activity, which transforms direct perception by adding a sign to it. For example, I see from afar an object all parts of which appear contracted and confused, without being able to distinguish any of them at the distance where I am; but if I happen to be informed in some way that it is such and such an object, the perception of which is familiar to me, I instantly distinguish its form, its size, etc. Why this sudden change in the power of the organ? Let a man approach or go away, I see him always as the same figure; why, when the optical angle varies, is the perception fixed?

If habit had not previously impressed on the mind images which are perpetually mingled and confused with real external appearances and which modify them in a thousand ways, one could undoubtedly determine according to the laws of optics, the limitations of distinct vision. But how far these limits retreat and vary according to our familiarity with the objects, according to the activity and the habits of the imagination! And how by disregarding these habits, could one conceive of the prodigious changes which must operate in the configuration and curvature of the eye to see distinctly at such different ranges?

Let us note that all these effects of the imagination, these judgments, these memories which give to perception its present form, vary with the promptitude and facility of the movements and activity of the external organ. Habit renders the judgments like the movements ever prompter and more unconscious and the activity of the individual ends by being transferred entirely to the external object. Color, form, distance, everything is accumulated on the solid core, confused in one impression, one indivisible sensation which the eye seems to receive naturally in opening to the light. Such is the great law of habit, of numberless operations and movements associated with each other and become extremely prompt and ready, producing weakening and disappearance of effort, insensibility in action, clearness and precision in its results.

Third, all that we have said in the two preceding articles should be applied to impressions of hearing and to vocal movements: it will suffice to note here the principal analogies.

The impressions of hearing are naturally successive like those of touch and habit teaches us likewise first to distinguish the individual terms which follow one another by as many movements; then to reunite them and to perceive accurately many together. It thus creates a harmony for the ear, as it creates a symmetry for touch, a parity of means and ends. In proportion as the vocal instrument is tuned and acquires determinations like those of hearing, the melodious sequence is more distinctly perceived. The speed of this can be indefinitely increased; the terms can mingle and combine with each other without being confused; soon the voice, by virtue of its habits, anticipates them, supplements them, or accompanies them; if hearing is struck by the treble, the voice can respond to it by the second part or bass. The sound of direct impression is separated internally from the harmonious sound of reflection and both when perceived together will be immediately distinguished much more easily externally. Let us note, nevertheless, that the ear becomes accustomed with more or less difficulty to the effects of harmony, while melody is a pleasure of all ages and places. Does not that too confirm our principles? The source of every distinction is in activity: without the vocal organ, the faculties of hearing would be extremely limited. Now, this primitive organ can never execute but one movement, one sound at once.

The exercise of touch and of progressive movement enters into the habits of hearing also, but this association has perhaps not all the effect that is attributed to it. We would in vain know and recognize that two sounds come from two different objects; we would confuse them no less, if the organ was not properly disposed and trained as we have just seen. We also learn by certain signs (which habit creates for us and then makes us confuse in the impression itself) to judge of the distance of the object from which comes such and such a noise, such and such a recognized sound, which strikes us. These very rapid judgments are more confused, less assured, grounded on a greater number of repetitions than those of sight, which correspond to them. But the mechanism is absolutely the same.

Finally, all our affective sensations even, provided that they are tempered to a certain point, are associated with the impression of resistance, with the exercise of our different movements, and when related to the external world or to parts of our body which are their seat, receive the feeble degree of information of which they are susceptible. Sometimes they take their place among the signs of the imagination, but it is most frequently to trouble and distract it. They enter into our judgments, but it is to confuse its terms. Their violent power dominates all, but leaves it in obscurity.

We have seen by what sequence of means, what repetitions of acts, our perceptive faculty is formed and developed; we have betaken ourselves to the creation of its first products in order to observe the simplest order of their combinations. Let us continue to examine how these products are extended and complicated through the repeated addition of new circumstances, what are the different orders of operations and of judgments which result from them, in short what habit can do to render these operations ever prompter and easier, these judgments more inflexible and more pertinacious, in order at last to blind the individual to the origin and number of the former and to the ground and legitimacy of the latter.

CHAPTER III

ASSOCIATED PERCEPTIONS AND THE DIVERSE HABITUAL JUDGMENTS WHICH RESULT FROM THEM

"Omnes perceptiones tam sensus, quam mentis, sunt ex analogia hominis, non ex analogia universi; est que intellectus humanus instar speculi ad radios rerum inaequalis, qui suam naturam naturae rerum immiscet, eamque distorquet et inficit."—(Bacon.)

The nature of the understanding is nothing other than the sum of the principal habits of the central organ, which must be considered as the universal sense of perception. The determinations characteristic of this organ and persisting in its very heart (*sein*), constitute that faculty which we called imagination. It is this which, reacting on the external senses and incessantly mingling its products with their impressions, becomes an uneven and mobile mirror, suited to transform the rays emanating from things and to modify their relations.

In proportion as the field of our perceptive faculty is extended and diversified, as the impressions are combined, as the operations and judgments are multiplied, the imaginary mirror acquires more influence, and it is by its reflected light far more than by the direct rays that we end by perceiving and contemplating objects.

We have already seen some of these elementary effects of imagination. Let us follow them into a higher order of associations and judgments.

PERCEPTIONS ASSOCIATED BY SIMULTANEITY

I. We can to all intents and purposes no more cease perceiving something which resists us, than cease feeling our own existence. The impression of effort is the principal and most profound of all our habits; it subsists while the other modifications pass and follow one another; it, therefore, coincides with all and furnishes them a base on which they are attached and fixed.

But effort presupposes two terms or rather a *subject* and an object essentially relative to each other. It is always the subject which is modified, but if it only made itself felt, it would remain identified with its modification and it itself would be unknown. It can not be known without being circumscribed, without being compared to its object. It is in the latter that it is perceived, that it is in some fashion mirrored. It is, therefore, to the object that it will relate alike all that it distinguishes and compares.

Such is the foundation of this relation of inherence of our more or less affective modifications (provided that they do not occupy the whole faculty of feeling) to the parts of the body which are its seat and especially of the unimportant and distinct impressions to the external and resistant support about which they gather. This is our earliest judgment and one that has become so profoundly habitual that nothing less than all the power of reflection is needed to wonder at it and to question its causes!

Our modifications associated by simultaneity with resistance and projected outside of us, are undoubtedly far from their simple and individual character. As *pure* sensations, they would be in some fashion isolated or without a common bond which unites them. As *qualities* of the *object*, they are grouped and crowded around it, strongly adhere to it and are combined in a single perception, represented externally by the resistant unity, in the same way that a series of simple units is reunited and determined by a single sign. And in fact, the natural sign fulfills the same office for the senses and the imagination as the artificial symbol for *memory* (as we shall see elsewhere).

Among these heterogeneous qualities whose number is increased by experience and whose association is cemented by habit, there is not one which cannot serve as a sign for all those which coöperate to form the same compound. It is sufficient that the central organ has contracted through the frequency of repetition the determinations necessary to reproduce their sum from the simple and repeated activity of one of the associated elements.   This is the same mechanism as that of which we have spoken (see preceding chapter) in the exercise of touch and sight.   But this function of sign does not belong equally to all the elementary impressions; habit attributes it sometimes in an exclusive manner to the one which has struck the organ more continually or which plays a more essential rôle in the total perception; the one in short on which attention is more particularly and more frequently fixed.   The *signs* of *habit* are ordinarily drawn from the forms and figures and colors; touch always furnishes the most certain and the least deceptive; that is the principal source of judgment and the basis of every good judgment; the eye gives the most superficial and the most trivial, whence a multitude of illusions.   The other senses take a less active, a less general part in our judgments; their signs are usually more uncertain and more confused.   But however accessory, however uncertain be the quality which fulfills the function of a sign, it can always by virtue of acquired habits and determinations persisting in the common center provoke the more or less energetic reaction of that center upon the external senses, thus drawing along mechanically the imaginary appearance of the ensemble of qualities or associated impressions, and if not their illusory perception, at least the real supposition of their co-existence.

Here is one of the principal bases of the experience which directs us, but also a too fertile source of prejudices which blind us.

Familiarized with the external appearances of the objects which have assiduously struck us, we judge quickly from the simplest of these appearances, the identity or similarity of their most inner properties without needing to verify them anew; we recognize them, we posit them without investigation, we see them by the imagination, even when they are concealed from the eye.

Thus, the experienced physician reads in an external sign all the prognoses and diagnoses of an illness; the chemist will tell without hesitation at the first inspection of a mineral, what is the number and nature of the elements which compose it; the painter embraces in one glance the whole effect of a picture or of a view; the musician sees and thinks that he simultaneously hears, in perusing a page of music, the harmonious effect of all the parts; the sailor with ordinary sight distinguishes a vessel in the obscure speck which advances from the boundaries of the horizon. . . . All believe that they see and directly feel what they imagine, judge and compare, so easy, prompt and certain has habit made these operations. Without doubt it is a good thing to judge quickly, but it is above all important to judge well and to see only what exists. Now, do the signs which are grounded only on habit always fulfill these essential conditions?

What relations, what close bonds exist between the external and superficial appearances which have always impressed us and these inner qualities which are revealed to our experiences in certain cases only? Because they are sometimes encountered together, can one affirm their necessary and certain coincidence? From the fact that they are associated in the imagination, does it follow that they are invariably united externally? Might not these same appearances be found again in essentially different compounds, or be lacking in some substances which are otherwise absolutely alike? What will be the errors, if through habit we conclude identity in the first case, diversity in the second; if we judge, for example, of the properties of gold by its yellow color; of the sweetness of sugar by its whiteness, etc.!

It is signs of habit which, abstracted in some manner from familiar perceptions and transferred to the midst of new and quite different forms, give to our first judgments a deceptive generality and begin to open the circle of error with that of knowledge. As the child, misled by some rough semblances in form, clothes, etc., applies to the stranger the tender name of father, so the man—still a child—extends his *ego* over the whole of nature, attributes his will, his own activity, to all that sustains with him the general relation of mobility, animates with his soul the stars, the clouds, the rivers, the plants and peoples with genii, with active powers, the sky and the earth.

The same principle of illusions follows us from the cradle to the complete development of our faculties. It is the habits of the imagination which almost always disfigure the simple sense reports, prejudice us as to the ground of things because of some familiar portion of the surface, as to the nature of objects because of our accustomed impressions, as to the identity of facts because of the faintest resemblances. It is habits which draw us along in a hastiness adverse to all examination, give us that blind confidence which cannot doubt or enquire, and thus perpetuate the errors and prejudices to which they have given birth. Through them all that is relative becomes absolute; what is circumscribed in one point of space and time is extended to all times and to all places. Thus, garbled experiences, facts isolated or imperfectly seen, acquire in the prejudiced imagination, which insists on reproducing the image of them, the generality and inflexibility of laws of nature.

We shall see in the following how artificial signs coöperate to extend and cement this order of habitual associations and judgments; it is sufficient here to have recognized their bases and indicated their general effects.

PERCEPTIONS ASSOCIATED IN THE ORDER OF SUCCESSION

II. When an impression is converted into a sign of habit, its renewed presence, so to say, brandishes the whole sheaf of those which are associated with it by simultaneity and the individual perceives instantly a multitude of qualities which he relates to the familiar object, although they are not actually comprized in it. Even if habit should permit him then to recover himself and to think of separating the products of his imagination from those of his senses, their instantaneousness, their perfect coincidence would often put an insuperable obstacle in the way. It is not quite the same with associations formed by the repetition of a certain successive order. Here the activity of the imagination, in some fashion being inserted in the interval which separates two terms of an habitual series, can isolate one from the other and be clear to the simplest reflection.

On the other hand, as most phenomena are unfolded to our senses in a successive order, it is principally upon this order that the habits of our imagination and of our judgments should be moulded. This class of habits is, therefore, at the same time the most numerous and the easiest to recognize.

If many impressions have succeeded each other a certain number of times in a constant and uniform order, the organ of thought will have contracted the determinations necessary to reproduce them in the same manner and with a precision, a regularity, an assurance which are always proportionate to the frequency of repetitions. The first impression or the first term of the series cannot, therefore, be reproduced without all the others being awakened successively and in the same order, as in a chain of which the links, although distinct from one another, are closely united, the impulsion communicated to the first is rapidly transmitted to the last of the row.

If we should suppose that the impulsion begins at one of the middle links of the chain, the movement would be diffused equally up and down toward the two extremes; likewise if any one term of the habitual series of impressions happens to be realized alone externally, it will not fail to awaken in the imagination all those which have preceded it (going backward to the first) as well as those which have directly followed. In considering any one term in relation to the one which follows it (or which the imagination always reproduces immediately after it by virtue of habit), this term is called or judged to be the *cause* and its follower is called or judged to be the *effect*. Thus, when we see a body moving, we imagine or suppose immediately a cause, that is to say another body which has struck against the former, and we thus go back from cause to cause to the hand which could have started the first movement, habit obstinately excluding any other cause of movement. Likewise if we see one body which approaches another, we suppose without hesitation or we imagine in advance, the movement which is going to be communicated to the latter, and this effect, for which we were prepared by so many antecedent repetitions, appears to us quite simple.

Habit creates for us causes in the order of succession, as essences in that of coexistents, and these relations of before and after which we call ideas of cause and effect, have their whole foundation in the determinations of the organ of thought subjected by habit to retracing our successive impressions in the same order according to which they have constantly been reproduced.

Fortified by a multitude of experiences, this habit acquires an irresistible predominance, becomes the spring of all our conduct, the determining cause of our daily actions. The constant succession of the same phenomena being represented, in fact, by a fixed and parallel series of images or determinations persisting in the internal sense, the first associated sign is sufficient to bring in advance the whole of those phenomena before the view of the imagination. Struck by those pictures, as by the very events which they report to us, we act, we prepare with confidence all our means of industry, now to profit by favorable influences, now to avert the pernicious effects of hostile causes. The appearance of the star of Syrius prepared ancient Egypt for the rich overflowing of the Nile; the ignorant sailor, like the enlightened disciple of Newton, reads in the phases of the moon the time of strong or weak tides; the simple country dweller judges without barometer of the approaching variations of the atmosphere and regulates all his work by the immutable order of the celestial revolutions. Everything becomes a *sign* in nature, because everything is connected through habit in the organ endowed with the faculty of perceiving phenomena and of conserving and reproducing their images.

But let us return to our series of familiar impressions. We

have likened their terms to contiguous links of a moving chain; and if one supposes in reality each impression represented by the corresponding movement of a fibre of the brain, one could imagine a sort of linkage between these fibres, the bonds of which habit would tighten, the connections of which it would make closer.

In this hypothesis, the activity communicated to the first or to any one of the fibres thus bound together would be rapidly transmitted to all the others and the individual would have a series of ideas or of inner representations which would be parallel and corresponding to the habitual order of perceptions which come to him from without. Now it may happen either that these last perceptions succeed each other in reality in the accustomed order as the individual imagines them and while he imagines them, or that when this order is suddenly changed, externally troubled, it opposes that of the brain habits, or finally that these habits have their free and spontaneous effect independently of every sign, of every outer provocation. We shall examine successively each of these three cases.

1. When the fibres are prepared for movement and pitched, so to say, to the tone of a series of familiar objects, the appearance of one of them alone suffices to bring back all the others. The brain outruns the external sense, reacts on it and shows it by a sort of reflection much more than it perceived directly. Each of the fibres having, therefore, taken by itself the movement which the action from without tended to communicate to it, when this action chances to be effected in the accustomed order, it will bring little change to the state of the fibre which, like a vibrating cord in action, must experience less change through the force which strikes it in the direction of its actual oscillations than through one which would arouse it from absolute rest. If there is less change, the impression will be weaker; but what is this weakening of an impression in the cerebral center? Is it a progressive degradation to the point of complete annihilation as in the case of simple sensation? No.

The repeated perception is not diminished, properly speaking; it merely becomes more indifferent and does not remain less uniformly susceptible of discrimination. When the carelessness of habit lets it escape, the voluntary act, which formed it, can frequently still retain it, revive it and render to it, if not its attraction, at least its original clarity.

The same mechanism explains to us, therefore, the promptitude, the facile succession of our repeated perceptions, as well as our indifference for their objects. We see also why every habitual effect, being accomplished in advance in the imagination, when it is realized externally, has no longer any power to move us or surprise us, why our senses slip over the surface of familiar objects with such an air of distraction (*consuetudine oculorum assuescunt animi, neque mirantur neque requirunt causas earum rerum quas semper vident*, Cicero, *Tuscul*). Again what is there, in fact, interesting about an object already seen many times? Why should the external sense still labour at exploring it in detail? What is the need, when the active imagination has completely comprehended it from the first warning of its presence? What motive is there, when apathetic indifference stifles all curiosity? This is why nature vainly displays to our accustomed eyes its most beautiful and imposing phenomena. Their order of succession is uniform, their gradations are well contrived; one is prepared to see them because one has always seen them, and what one sees always prepares for what must follow.

Facility, rapidity, indifference, therefore, are the three concomitant results of habit, as long as the perceived order remains parallel to the imagined order.

2. But while the imagination, warned by the first external sign, hastens to realize the accustomed series before the slower organ has been able to grasp its terms, if an interruption, a change in the familiar order, intervenes from without, the fibre, the vibrating cord in animation is suddenly arrested in its oscillations; an impulsive force tends to impress contrary movements upon it, its condition is changed, its sensibility excited.

According to the degree of opposition, the greatness or the vivacity of the contrasts, the pleasure or the pain connected with the previous condition, the importance of the expected effect, or according only to the age of the habit, the rapidity and the force with which it draws along the fibres in their movements, the imagination in its downward course, the individual will be struck with surprise, astonishment, admiration, fear, terror, or fright.

Thus it is that every new phenomena, every suspension, every change in an order which has become familiar to us, arouses our attention and our sensibility enervated by habit. If the constant order of nature, if the regular course of those spheres which are balanced in space, if the too uniform products of the compounds which we submit to our experience, can cool our curiosity, deaden our ardour and our need of knowledge, real or apparent anomalies in this reputed invariable order, extraordinary facts, unforseen combinations, offered frequently by happy chances, render the human spirit active, snatch it from its lethargy and push it still further in the endless career which lies open to its perfectibility. How many investigations and labors and discoveries are going to be connected with a single new fact which finds itself in opposition with the system of ideas and habits of a century! It is even more by its apparent digressions than by its regular course that nature invites us to study her and teaches us to know her.

In order to stir and please us, it is ever necessary also to draw us gently outside of this circle of too narrow, too uniform impressions in which habit restrains and fastens us. That is the whole secret of the fine arts. It is in contriving surprises for our senses, in creating for us new manners of seeing and hearing that the painter and musician delight us. Notice especially with what art this clever composer knows how to deceive the habits of the ear, to excite it with unexpected modulations, to draw it further from the repose toward which it gravitates, in order to make its sweetness better enjoyed!

Surprise, more or less vivid emotion, when the perceived

order is contrary to the imagined order, is the second effect which is proportionate to the force and persistency of the habits.

3. Since, in a series of familiar impressions, imagination plays the principal rôle, and since it is to the play of habit, rather than to the actual exercise of the external sense, that all the preceding effects are due, these effects will still be, therefore, almost the same, if in removing every sign, every outside cause of provocation, we suppose that the chain of fibres, prepared for movement, effectuates its determinations either spontaneously or by some inner impetus.   Facility, insuperable tendency to imagine objects in the order and rank in which they habitually succeed each other and, by reason itself of the number and frequency of their repetitions, difficulty of isolating terms from each other, their quick succession, which prevents examining them in detail and appreciating their number and quality; indifference, which actually removes them from the activity of the will, but the possibility subsisting (in spite of habit) of rendering to these immediate products of perceptive activity their original distinctness, if the will is so determined; oppositions, contrasts between the series of habitual ideas and others of not such long standing; surprises, emotions, struggles, allurements in the contrary direction where habit has so much the more force as its influence is less perceived; hallucinations, illusions of every sort . . . . The inner scene is only the repetition of that which takes place externally, and the individual himself is his own theatre.   We shall soon see how imagination can have its own habits independent of those of the external world; but we must still consider the two representative and perceptive faculties in their reciprocal relation and influence.

COMPARISON OF HABITUAL IMPRESSIONS WITH IMAGES—JUDG-
MENTS DERIVED FROM IT

III. When one of the impressions associated in a series or a whole serves as a sign for the total perception, the latter, contemplated as if through reflection in the imaginary mirror, frequently attracts only the most superficial attention; the individual casts on the familiar object the hasty and thought-less glance of indifference and goes on.   This glance, thought-less as it is, is none the less sufficient to recognize the object as *being the same* as the one which has so many times struck the sight.   Now, this recognition presupposes one or perhaps many infinitely prompt comparisons (and indifference itself, in this case, presupposes judgment).

Does one wish to be assured that these operations, although unperceived, really exist?   Let one imagine some change in the form or position of the object known.   In slurring over it with its ordinary rapidity, the senses will immediately perceive the change and stop in their course; but the relation of *otherness* presupposes indeed that of previously perceived identity.

How, therefore, do we recognize that an object is the same or that it has changed?   On what is this judgment founded? How does it escape us in certain cases to the point of being merged with the impression itself?

Let us first take an example where the judgment is revealed through its tardiness and we shall immediately see how it becomes insensible by its rapidity.

When after a long absence I see again a face whose features, formerly familiar to me, have undergone in the course of time great alterations, what likeness this face still keeps to its former self can serve as a sign to my imagination and retrace the former image there.   At the instant that this reproduction takes place, a detailed comparison is established—feature by feature—between the copy and the model, which makes me affirm the personal identity of the individual and judge at the same time of all the changes which have taken place in him. "It is indeed he!"   I shall cry to myself, "but *quantum mutatus ab illo!*"   It is very evident here that *reminiscence* is founded upon a real comparison between the image and the object; it is also combined there with circumstances of place and time which, compared in memory and perception, give a new weight to judgment.

When the object has not ceased to be familiar and when it offers no sensible trace of alteration, its identity can equally be recognized only through comparison. But, in the first case, the terms of the relation were distinct and separate; they succeeded each other with effort and slowness. Here the object and its image, the accessories of perception, the circumstances associated in the memory, tend to be merged through their resemblance, their proximity, and the extreme rapidity of their succession. Comparison will, therefore, be unconscious (*insensible*). Thus habit influences memory as well as all other operations which it reveals to us by their increasing promptitude and facility.

We can see, by what precedes, the reason why we are so little struck by changes and disfigurements which take place slowly either in us or in the beings with whom we walk in the course of existence. This is why we always take for the term of comparison, the image which is nearest and freshest in the memory. Moreover we do not perceive any contrast and that explains further to us our indifference to all that is familiar. On the contrary, when one sees again after a long time objects formerly known, one is indeed more keenly affected than if they were quite new. This is because their recognition is founded upon many very striking points of comparison, which give occasion for the display of our activity. It is because the individual, importuned by the numerous memories which happen to be inserted between two distant points of his existence, gathers round the same object all the modifications that its presence awakes. This is why the sensitive Rousseau cried after thirty years: "There is some periwinkle!"[1]

[1] *Les Confessions*, Book VI. She (Madame de Warens) was in a sedan chair and I followed on foot. The road ascended: she was rather heavy and fearing to tire the porters, she wanted to get down when we had gone almost half way and go the rest of the distance on foot. While walking she saw something blue in the hedge, and said to me: "There is some periwinkle still in bloom." I had never seen periwinkle, I did not stoop to examine it and I am too near-sighted to distinguish from my height plants on the ground. I cast only a glance on it in passing and almost thirty years passed without my seeing periwinkle again

To the judgment which makes us recognize objects, is ordinarily joined another which, either through habit or through the manner in which it affects us, is still more apt to be merged with the impression itself. I wish to speak of that judgment (others would say that feeling) which makes us find objects beautiful or ugly. The qualities which we express by these terms are indeed generally less relative to the first laws of our sensibility than to habits acquired by our imagination. Without examining whether there exists an absolute *beautiful* founded upon these laws, let us observe, as to habits, that our ideas of *beauty* are not at all, as they say, *archetypes*, but traced upon certain impressions chosen at first from among those which are most familiar to us. The imagination subsumes these ideas under the form of different more or less fixed groups. Then when an object happens to strike the senses, it is compared to the group, to the ideal model which corresponds to it and judged beautiful or ugly, according as it has more qualities similar or contrary to this model. Habit gives to these comparisons, which are sometimes very numerous, its ordinary promptitude and facility. Then one judges of beauty as one feels, as one *tastes* a flavor.

Since this prototype which we name *ideal beauty* is first composed of sense impressions, it must vary with all that occasions them, such as climates, places, customs, degrees of sensibility of nations and individuals.

If sometimes a sort of instinct of the beautiful, the great, the sublime in all the genres, seems to draw the genius outside of the narrow circle of real objects, in order to transport him

---

or paying any attention to it. In 1764, being at Cressier with my friend Monsieur de Peyrou, we were climbing a little mountain at the summit of which he has a pretty summer house which he appropriately calls Belle-Vue. I then began to search a little for plants. While climbing and looking among the bushes, I uttered a cry of joy: "Ah, there is some periwinkle!" and that is what it was indeed. De Peyrou saw the joy, but he was ignorant of its cause. He will find out some day I hope when he reads this. The reader may judge, by the impression of such a little object, of the impression which everything related to the same epoch has made on me.

into an imaginary world, the elements of which he creates, orders, polishes, elaborates at his will, habit restrains him still in his excursions as by a central force.   It is ever the colors of the sky of his native country which present themselves under his brushes; it is his native land which furnishes the raw material from which he constructs his enchanted palaces.   This beautiful nature which he conceives, which he appears to discover, is still only the embellished copy of that which struck his first glances and gave the impulse to his budding sensibility.

How many judgments and operations enter into the exercise of this function of perceiving, which appears simple to us now! The term *sensation*, confusedly appropriated by all its products, is itself a speaking proof of what habit can do, in order to hide from us the number and kind of acts that it directs.   Although we have insisted at length on this subject, we are undoubtedly still far from having revealed plainly all the elements; but we may conclude from this chapter and the one which precedes that in the present condition of our faculties, every perception is composed of more or less numerous judgments of habit; that these judgments, these comparisons which escape us are founded on a similar mechanism: the external sense gives the first information, the first sign, the first term of the relation; the inner organ reacts with its acquired determinations, furnishes the other terms—the most influential ones, since they give to the perception its principal character.   Habit has for its purpose to bring these terms together and to render their succession infinitely prompt and easy.   Then the individual, ignoring what happens in himself, transfers his activity, his own force, to the resisting object and clothes it with all that of which he is robbed.

CHAPTER IV

SENSORY HABITS AND HABITS OF THE IMAGINATION

We saw finally that our perceptions, our ideas and the different judgments that we form about the coexistence or succession of familiar objects, about identity, resemblance, change, contrast, beauty, ugliness, were accompanied or followed, in their original manifestation, by certain more or less affective modifications which we call surprise, admiration, fear, joy or sadness. These modifications which follow the act of judgment and appear inseparable from it, ought nevertheless to be distinguished by an exact analysis which shall separate all that habit confounds together. When these modifications are considered in their psychological aspect, they are called feelings of the soul; we shall retain this name for them, since it depicts their essentially affective character and ranks them in a different class from that of simple sensations which are independent of all judgment and with which we cannot confuse them. As composite products of the sensitive function, the feelings of which we speak must be subject to the same alterations of habit as the simple and isolated products which have already occupied us (in the first chapter of this memoir).

In fact we have already noticed, and our experience confirms it at every instant, that these different emotions of surprise, fear, admiration, etc., are never excited except by new and unusual objects or objects which strike us after a long interval; all affective feeling vanishes (although the perception remains unchanged) through familiarity with the same objects, or in proportion as the imagination is accustomed to foresee or foreshadow them in advance, in proportion, in short, as judgments become more assured, easier, prompter.

This evanescence, this diminution of every conscious effect

appears therefore to be a law of habit as constant and universal as that of the increasing rapidity and ease of the results of our motor activities; and in applying these two laws together to all phenomena that reflection reveals in us, there seems not to be one of them which cannot serve them as proof and confirmation.

How does it happen, however, that certain feelings acquire a singular vivacity and energy when the ideas fitted to excite them are more frequently reproduced? How does it happen that these ideas themselves preserve all their brilliance and sometimes become more attractive through repetition? Why do they suddenly resume their predominance after having lost it through familiarity? What, then, is this Proteus of habit which escapes us when we think we have grasped it, which now blunts, now irritates our sensibility, now weakens, now revivifies our modifications?

In order to reconcile these contradictions and to try to recognize the causes of these noteworthy anomalies in the ordinary results of habit, let us first examine what is the nature of those ideas and feelings of which the potency resists the changes of time and the most frequent repetitions, and increases through its very duration. We shall in the second place examine what are the organic states which coöperate to nourish and sometimes to produce these feelings and ideas.

This subject, treated at length and as it deserves to be, would be beyond our competency, and would also exceed the limits in which we must confine ourselves. Let us try only to grasp the points of contact which it may have with the question which occupies us and with the purpose which we have set before us.

I. So long as ideas are really images and remain clearly delimited in thought, as are the external objects which have served as their models and to which they may be constantly compared, the effects of habit and repetition on these ideas and on the determinations which correspond to them, falling under the simple and ordinary cases which we have studied, may always be conceived and represented in some manner under definite forms.   Experiences are not lacking to confirm them positively nor expressions to describe them.

But, if it is of ideas or rather phantoms (*phantasmata*, as Hobbes calls them) which are vague and undetermined in their nature, connected with entities either real or imaginary, but beyond the reach of the senses; potent excitants of fear or hope, beguiling or frightening the imagination, of which they are the work, by colors and forms now gracious, now sinister and terrible, it is plain that these ideas, these sentiments, the seat of which is entirely internal, must form, through their persistance, a class of habits separated from those which arise and are maintained by the constant activity of the same external causes, by the uniform and repeated exercise of our perceptive faculty.   The mechanism of these habits is also much more difficult to grasp.   Their results are better felt than conceived and perhaps one conceives them better than one can express them.   Let us recur to examples and choose first the most remarkable.   They will furnish us with all the enlightenment of which the subject is susceptible.

1. The imagination seems to tend, by a sort of instinct, to the production of superstitious ideas of every kind.   Bound by intimate relations to the sensory functions, the impulsion of which it follows, independent of the will to which it dictates rather than submits, this faculty demands, craves in some way, the nutriment which suits it.   It has an affection for the marvelous, eagerly pursues all that is hidden from the senses and covered with a veil, all that flatters a blind tendency to credulity, an ever increasing need of strong and profound emotions.

The history of the errors, of the strange and atrocious follies of the human mind, from the birth of societies to their old age, sufficiently proves the power and universal predominance of illusions, of superstitious beliefs and practises of every kind, the energy and impetuosity of the feelings and the obstinacy and persistance of the habits which are connected with this origin.

The fear of invisible powers, *which arises from ignorance of natural causes*, must be at first the most powerful of fears; the hope which has the same basis must also predominate over all hopes; for the vivacity and duration of feelings is ever proportioned to the unlimited extent of perspectives, to the distance of the objects, to the vagueness and indeterminateness of the ideas which correspond to them.

After mysterious pictures and all the effects of superstitious delirium begin to be established in the imagination (and they are formed and developed there especially in consequence of certain primitive tendencies of temperament or of acquired tendencies which have become habitual), they fill it, obsess it unceasingly, leave it no respite. The same images, the same sentiments, the same practises, far from being made lukewarm by the ordinary influence of habit, on the contrary become the more potent; be it charm or worry, there is a need and an ever more pressing need to attend to it. Absorbed in the same group of stimuli, the individual returns to them every day with more force and obstinacy, ceaselessly summons them and no longer can or will be distracted from them. These phantoms, inherent in thought, the *idols* (*idola mentis*) of which they become, seem to be for its organ what artificial habitual stimulants are for the organs of sensation; there is the same necessity, the same restlessness, the same need of exaggerating the impressions with which habit alone has connected a feeling of existence which incessantly tends to be revived.

See in fact how these gloomy fanatics love ever to darken the colors of their pictures. They stir themselves up to fear as well as to suffer, they refine on a grief which is losing its sting, as Sybarites on a pleasure which takes its flight.

All continued or repeated exacerbation of sensibility, whatever be the inner seat or spring, must, in fact, have parallel results which correspond to one another in the sensations and in the sentiments of the soul, in the physical and mental aspects of our being. But, when the cause acts directly on the very source of sensibility, without foreign or external perturbation, the effects must be more intense and varied, the habits more profound and obstinate.

2. Every passion is a sort of superstitious worship rendered to an imaginary object or to one which, even though real, emerges from the domain of the perceptive faculty in order to go over entirely to that of the imagination. This object is always more or less concealed and indefinite; it presents itself at a certain distance and under many different aspects; it puts successively into play the forces of fear and hope: in order to attain it, there must be numerous obstacles, difficulties, chances to be encountered . . . . such is the primary spring of the passions which tyrannize over us. That is the cause of the fixity and the increasing energy of the ideas to which they give rise and of the feelings which they excite.

It is the vague, unlimited perspectives, the perils, the risks, the shifting chances of ambition and glory; it is the ideal charm of enjoyments allied to great power, a great strength of position which first entices so many men into this brilliant career and immediately keeps them there through necessity and habit in spite of disgust and failure. Again it is all this vagueness of desires, fears, and hopes, these obstacles to overcome, these ideas of power which nourish the love of gambling and avarice and make them insatiable (*crescit indulgens sibi dirus hydras nec sitim pellit*—Horace).

Habit, in all cases, far from withering the imagination, on the contrary renders the same springs of its activity more dear to it; obstinately fixes it in the same direction and rivets the chains which keep it enslaved there; but while the end is one, there is a great variety of means in a single sort of excitation, a host of different modes. The frame of the imaginary picture may indeed be stationary, but it is like a moving picture, the successive figures of which are grouped and combined in a thousand ways; there is no continuity of impressions there, no monotomy, no uniform repetition.

It is perhaps always the same image which pursues the young lover; but with how many varying accessories is his active imagination pleased to color it! The man of ambition contemplates in a higher position, the conqueror sees in glory, the miser in his gold, the representation of a multitude of goods, advantages, enjoyments, which are infinitely diversified; for the imaginary world is limitless. . . . . Thus, on the one hand chained by habit, on the other hand free in its excursions, the imagination finds in its appropriate activity all that can at once flatter two general tendencies, the contrast of which makes harmony in the mental world; the one, the principle of movement which gives the active being the perpetual need of changing; the other, the force of inertia, restraining the weak and limited being within the narrow circle of habits.

3. As long as the obstacles succeed each other and the goal is distant while at the same time ever promising attainment, the conscious being who lives by movement as by the air that he breathes, enjoys his activity, his desires, his hopes; his feelings are immune from the weakening effect of habit. But after the object is attained, if the imagination sees nothing further, if possession is peaceful, uniform, uncontested, the seductive prism is broken, the charm is destroyed, and habit resumes its sway. It is a general law of our sensibility, whatever be the modes of its exercise, that it can never be fixed at the same point, persist at the same pitch; it must ever rise, *et in altum vehitur* . . . . , *nec reperit locum consistendi* (hence comes all that we are, good as well as bad). If sensibility tends to rise progressively, the uniform object, possessed without opposition, which no longer furnishes it the means of such heightening will cease to fill it; but it is when habituation causes it to find the same food more insipid, that it in fact renders it more necessary. Here we return to all that we have already said concerning sensations weakened in the organs but become necessary for the sensory system. The organic cause is doubtless the same in both cases; but what a difference in the results! How complicated are the effects! How much more energetic are the feelings because of the reaction of the internal sense, the number and the variety of the associated ideas!

The too familiar object which we are on the point of losing, again passes over entirely to the sway of the imagination. Suddenly stopped in a descent that habit has scooped out and rendered so easy, it is awakened, surprised and irritated by unexpected resistance and reacts with all the force of a long compressed spring. It is then that it invokes all its impressions, but lately so weak and languishing, gives them a new life, confers an illusory charm on the object which no longer exists, exaggerates the picture of past happiness, in order to render the privation of it more cruel.

Thus habit conceals from us under a mask of indifference the force of the bonds that it has woven. In order to know these bonds it is necessary to try to escape them, it is necessary to feel them relax and break!

These two beings, this husband and wife who have passed their life together, do not perhaps feel anything more than a very calm and feeble sentiment for each other. Age, time, habit have restricted its expansive power; but if cruel death happens to break these ancient ties, the unfortunate one who survives rejects an existence which has lost its support, follows the bier which carries away the cherished remains and soon mingles his own with them.

Tired of the monotonous life of the country where he was born, this restless youth goes to seek new impressions under another sky and in other climates. But soon he sees again in imagination the places to which his early habits call him. It is always to them that his thought wanders. Nothing can interest him, nothing can distract him. The unhappy man wastes away by slow degrees and succumbs under the weight of homesickness!

Of how many modifications and degrees of force and persistence, therefore, are these habits of the imagination and of feeling susceptible, according as the object is real or illusory, naked or wrapt in mysterious clouds, simple or varied, absent or present, free of every obstacle or surrounded by resistance! . . . .

It is in noting such differences in the very nature of the objects or ideas that one can reconcile many contradictions and explain many noteworthy anomalies in the ordinary effects of habit.   But, in order to succeed in clarifying this important subject, let us again see how the imagination may take on one steady direction; how the ideas and sentiments keep an inexhaustible vivacity and energy in consequence of certain more or less constant tendencies either of the organ of thought or of sensible centers on which it reacts and which irradiate towards it.

II. Independently of all acquired determination, the organ of thought sometimes draws from its own depths, pictures, series, combinations of ideas, which are not connected with any kind of model furnished by the habits of the senses or by previously acquired habits of the imagination.

These products, in a manner anomalous, may be only spurts of cerebral sensibility, passing glimmers, which, having no common link with the chain of habitual ideas, will not exercise any lasting influence on the state of thought and will leave no trace in memory.   Thus a man when he awakes in the morning forgets the witticisms which the fumes of wine the evening before caused to spring into his mind.   The most charming dreams disappear on waking; and these brilliant and extraordinary ideas, sometimes produced by a cloud of excitement, become absolutely foreign to the individual when he has returned to his natural state and is under the sway of his habits.

But it may also occur that these fantastic images acquire consistency through their duration and are transformed into obstinate habits, whose influence will be extended over the whole mass of acquired ideas and will sunder their chain and prejudice judgment forever.

This transformation of the products of mental excitement into persisting habits may take place in three principal ways: first, by the continuance of any cause, which acts directly and intimately upon the cerebral organ; in the second place, by the association of the fantastic image with the real objects or ordinary ideas which repeating themselves reproduce it incessantly and which it degrades by mingling with it; in the third place, by the fixed tendencies of an inner organ or of a sensible center, which first stimulated by the image produced in the mind, reacts in its turn to sustain it there. Let us rapidly run over these three cases.

1. The spontaneous activity of the mind or the anomalous cause which acts in its midst may be sufficiently energetic and continuous to impress on its products all the force, duration and consistency of real objects; and then the perceptions of the external senses would disappear before these products or taking on their colors, would be unable to reveal them in their true light and divert us from them. Judgments made upon real existence and the relations of these images have an inflexibility; feelings which result from them have an energy which nothing can balance, weaken or distract. As long as the inner seat is nourished by the same cause (*Tant que le foyer intérieur sera alimenté par la même cause*), habit will not have any direct influence on its products; only it will contribute much to aggravate its activity, to incorporate it more firmly in the cerebral system and to render it more rebellious to mental or physical curative means, which art may oppose to it.

2. Strange and singular ideas may sometimes arise suddenly in the sanest heads through the effect alone of the activity and momentary states of the brain. These ideas, at first not striking, may be mingled and associated with sense impressions. They will acquire through them a certain consistency, will assume a place in the regular series and combinations of judgments, will carry a germ of illusions and errors there, which, being developed through the frequent repetition of the same operations or judgments, will produce habits so much the more obstinate as their source is less suspected and more hidden in the depths of the human organism.

How many errors, miscalculations, paradoxes, vain hypotheses are there which owe their birth and tenacity to no other cause! And if the philosopher, who is most on guard against illusions of the inner sense, who, through the nature of the ideas with which he is occupied, must be least exposed to them, cannot always flatter himself that his habitual judgments are quite free from them, what will it be with regard to these unruly imaginations which deliver themselves with so much confidence to all phantoms, repulse the light of analysis which would tend to dispel them, nourish themselves solely on illusions, and finally have accustomed their brain to this sort of artificial stimulation, the effects of which we have already examined?   It is these visions, at first produced by a passing excitement, but immediately transformed into habits by assiduous contemplation or frequent repetition, which end by wholly unsettling the imagination of the devout person who believes himself such and such a saint sent by God or God himself; of the woman who identifies herself with such and such a heroine of romance; of that fool of Athens who considered all the vessels of the Piraeus his property, etc.

It seems, therefore, that if the spontaneous activity of the cerebral organ sometimes furnishes some sort of raw material for fantastic images, it is the continual preoccupation, the attention at first voluntary which the individual has been able to give them, it is particularly their association with external, familiar objects, which furnish them frequently with the opportunity of being reproduced and which fix and incorporate them afterwards in thought.   Also, one of the most powerful means of correcting these aberrations is to remove carefully all the sensible impressions, which, through a direct or indirect relation, would be able to restore the causes of them and nourish, through repetition, a disordered imagination; and that proves at the same time how difficult it must be to divert those obstinate images which are grounded on a supernatural order of things.

We may observe in the sequel all that the free repetition of linguistic signs adds to the diverse products of the imagination, which we have pointed out in this chapter.   Let us end by examining the part which the states of the internal organs play in it.

3. Every impression, every slightly energetic activity, which begins in any organ, is more or less obscurely transmitted to the different parts of the organism, through the intermediary of the center which in general serves them for a support, for communication, and through which in some manner passes their resultant. Reciprocally, sensory activity, which begins with a certain degree of force in the brain, is communicated and reflected to all parts and particularly to the centers and principal seats of sensibility, which contract and retain more or less firmly particular tendencies or determinations. It is thus that all the impressions are combined and are perpetually exchanged with each other, participate in the same individuality and are covered by a common judgment. It is thus that all the habits—the principal and necessary as well as the secondary and accidental—are grounded, extended and confirmed. Hence also, doubtless, comes in great part what is called the action and the reaction of the physical upon the mental, that is to say, the vivid images that the organ of thought produces by its activity or in consequence of its habits upon the affections and conditions of the internal organs, and these fixed conditions upon the nature, the vividness and the duration of the images.

It can, in fact, be scarcely doubted that the appearance of such and such ideas wakes and, in a certain manner, adjusts such and such internal organs which, acting in their turn on the brain, revive and maintain the same ideas.

This reciprocity of influence and even the priority of the activity of the parts or seats of sensibility, situated outside of the cerebral organ, are manifested in all the inclinations and operations of instinct; but when we are outside of nature and under the sway of artificial needs, the imagination in its turn precedes and anticipates the organic activity which must put it into play, and it is upon the habits proper to this faculty that the artificial bent which the organism receives and keeps, frequently depends. Thus obscene images, rather than an impelling necessity to fulfill the natural desire, too frequently, in a corrupt society, determine the premature and artificial stimulation of the sixth sense; this center acquiring a sinister predominance, through the frequent reproduction of the same images, may in its turn contribute to raise them and thus foment physical and moral depravity.   The cares and disturbance of an artificial life, the torments of a boundless ambition, the vain terrors of superstition, the devouring and unquenchable thirst of avarice, etc., are first grounded on certain ideal views which the captivated imagination is never wearied of contemplating; but the intense application of the brain, and such a mode of habitual application, excites sympathetically the activity of the sensible centers with which it puts itself in harmony, troubles the natural order of their functions, determines in them a lasting state of contraction or spasm, makes congestions arise there, etc.   These conditions, brought on by the habits of the imagination, become in their turn causes, powerfully influence the faculties of thought, impress a force, a direction, a uniform color upon all its products.   Such is, doubtless, one of the principal causes of the increasing energy, persistence, and incorruptibility of the ideas which tend to be connected with some dominant passion.   Thus habit, which blights the imagination and paralyses feeling, in the continuous or repeated activity of the same external causes, has (in this connection) no power over the immediate products of an inner mechanism, which is strengthened by its very continuance. *Viresque acquirit eundo.*

Therefore in comparing the ideas, tendencies, and habits which arise from these two kinds of causes, to wit, from the repeated activity of the external senses or from the experience and the conscious will on the one hand, from the characteristic and spontaneous activity of the brain, particularly when activated by the fixed states of the internal organs, on the other, we would clearly recognize, by the energy and the duration of the effects, the predominance of these latter causes.   And how could we resist the whole multitude of proofs which incessantly make them known to the same inmost sense?   What is it which determines such variable modes which we experience in the feeling of our existence, in the activity and deportment of all our faculties at different times, different seasons of the year, and often at each hour of the day? Whence comes it that our intellectual habits, formed so painfully and slowly, sometimes suddenly stand ineffectual? What do these tendencies signify, these obstinate ideas, which on the contrary suddenly engross all our imagination, persist in spite of will, and usurp the place of the most longstanding habits? Why does an analogous condition of the organism, returning at corresponding periods of life, give the freshness of novelty to old ideas which we no longer expected and revives habits which we considered obliterated? Why do a certain inertia in the organ of thought and a tendency to pursue obstinately the same system of ideas, always coincide with the tendencies of other organs to retain and fix in them the impressions which come to them from accidental causes or which are inherent in their vitality, those habits, for example, so tenacious in old age, those affections so lively in childhood, etc.?

These facts (and a multitude of others which I omit) are so striking, they have such intimate points of contact with all the habits of thought in general, in short they form such an important branch of their history that I thought I might be permitted this kind of digression, if such it is, in their favor. I now return to the investigation of purely ideological phenomena and of *active* habits, which are connected with the use of artificial signs.

ACTIVE HABITS

OR

The Repetition of the Operations which Are Based upon The Use of Voluntary and Articulated Signs

CHAPTER I

THE ASSOCIATION OF ARTICULATED SIGNS WITH THE DIFFERENT IMPRESSIONS; THE FOUNDATION OF DIFFERENT KINDS OF MEMORY

We have distinguished, in the Introduction of this work, two general classes of *signs*: one, which is composed of all the voluntary movements associated by nature itself and from the very first with sensible impressions which they serve to distinguish, to fix, and to *recall*; that is the principal fundation of *memory*. The other, which is formed of all impressions whatsoever, associated by habit in a single group or series, each of which, in being renewed, has power to reproduce all the others; that is the chief motive power of the *imagination*. The sigr s of the imagination are not at all free. It is an object external to the individual or a cause foreign to his will, which always fulfils this function, and habit itself prevents him from noticing it because of the singular promptitude and facility which it makes him acquire. The signs of the memory are free in principle (by their very nature); but habit still transforms them, changes their nature and nullifies their functions, since it makes them insensible. It is thus (see Chapter II, first part) that we do not recognize all the source of images or visual representations in primary resistance, and the functions of the signs or movements which have first served to put them into prominence in the external world. Further, it is thus that habit hides from us the necessary intervention of vocal movements in the discrimination and recall of our auditory impressions. Such, therefore, is the general effect of habit in the progressive development of our primitive faculties. It tends incessantly to bring together and merge two kinds of impressions which in their nature are distinct. It hides from the individual, with its characteristic activity, the difference which separates simple sensation from perception and judgment. Finally, it converts even the voluntary signs of recall into passive signs of the imagination.

When the perceptive faculty has attained this degree of improvement on the one hand and of blindness in its exercise on the other, the individual then remains passively given over to the impulsion from external causes, which frequently move him without his being conscious of it, or to organic tendencies, to involuntary spurts of sensibility, to the periodic rebirth of the same needs, which momentarily wake him from his lethargy only to plunge him back into it the instant afterwards. Circumscribed in a circle of operations which are always repeated in the same manner, he executes them without thinking of them, distractedly and as if in a sort of somnambulism. If he has a capacity for reflection, a power to react on everything that surrounds him and to be modified himself, this power is disguised by habit, by the facility and spontaneity of the first movements, or natural signs, on which it is grounded. In order to pass from the virtual to the actual, the individual must be determined to do deliberately all that he previously did through habit; he must go back to the source of his signs, unravel their functions, re-establish them by an act of his will, associate them firmly through a series of (deliberate) repetitions with all the sense impressions, all the products of thought, all that he perceives, all that he feels in himself and outside of himself. Here an endless task is opened to perfectibility; let us try to follow the first steps of an intelligent being in it and discover how habit may alternately serve him and harm him. We have seen what the results of this power are, when it dominates exclusively; let us now see it struggling with reflection.

I shall suppose an isolated individual who, arrived at the point where his perceptive faculty would have acquired through repeated exercise the ordinary development of which it is susceptible through the mere education from *things*, would suddenly feel the need of reflecting about himself and would conceive, as if by inspiration (for the determining cause makes no difference to the purpose that I have in view), the plan of starting the training of his senses over again, of henceforth maintaining a close communication with his thought, of observing all its progress, while guarding against that facility, that habitual automatism, the effects of which are revealed to him.

This individual will, therefore, begin by giving particular attention to the exercise of each of his senses, for it is only from this source that enlightenment can come to him. He will not be long in recognizing and distinguishing certain impressions, which he coöperates in giving to himself, which he in some manner creates by his own activity, from others in which he is or feels himself to be absolutely passive and modified in spite of himself. He will further notice, after some reflection, that the primary impressions are those that he distinguishes from each other the best. Even when the external cause has disappeared, he feels in himself the power to recall them by reacting on the organs which were their seat; and, replacing them as they were in perception, he also observes (when he surprises himself in states of reverie) that the images or copies of these impressions, and particularly those of sight, are clearly retraced without his recalling them, while those which have most vividly affected him and which awake his desires, do not arise even confusedly except when the discomfort of want makes itself felt. At all other times they remain as unrepresentable in memory as they were vague and, so to say, turbulent in sensation.

In *recalling* and *imagining* (which he does not confuse any more than *feeling* and *perceiving*), the individual who reflects and never loses sight of himself has observed that the images are connected or grouped together, in their voluntary or spontaneous reproduction, as the objects are or were externally. In recalling, for example, the form of the object which he has touched or in imitating noises and sounds that he has heard, he reproduces by the same act many other contemporaneous impressions which he did not have in view, of which he no longer even thought, and which consequently he would not have been able to recall directly if they had not been united with those which he had ready. Precious discovery indeed! for henceforth reflection shows him that he has only to imitate voluntarily—either by the repetition of the same circumstances or mentally—what happened, to bind (by a common and repeated attention) modifications and certain ideas to movements and impressions which are always in his power, in order to make the former participate in the same activity which directs the latter, and to acquire over his thought the same power that he exercises on his motor organs and through them on external nature.

Among the different movements or signs which he may choose to accomplish this great plan, he will be struck especially by those of the voice, the exercise of which had already been determined by nature and a primitive instinct of imitation. These signs are the nearest to him, the most convenient, the most appropriate for his purpose. When he exercises the vocal organ intentionally, his ego seems to divide into two distinct persons who are in communication. One speaks, the other listens; one executes movement, the other judges its execution, perceives in detail its effects, reaps its products. No impression, no other movement enjoys to this degree a double knowledge. None fulfils so perfectly the function of sign, favors solitary meditation, turns thought back upon itself in such an intimate manner. None is thus retained in the mind and procures that sort of sonorous electrification. Finally, no kind of sign is susceptible of that variety of characters, inflections, and tones which can lend itself to all sorts of imitations and portrayals, can satisfy all the needs of thought, guide it and follow it in the formation of its most complex pictures as well as in the details of its most delicate analyses.

Such is the justification of the preference which must be granted to the signs of the voice over all the other movements at our disposal, as soon as a beginning of experience, joined to reflection, would have caused us to have a presentiment of its advantages.

Our fictitious being is, therefore, going to work to give names to the different objects which he perceives, to the modifications which he experiences, to register thus all his experiences and to procure for himself the most efficacious means of recalling them and of keeping account of them.

As our only object is to rediscover in the earliest associations of linguistic signs with ideas, and in the manner in which these associations are performed, the ground and source of the different habits of memory, we shall here omit all the details which would divert us from this purpose and limit ourselves to some essential remarks.

In the *vocal sounds* which the individual attaches to the objects of perception or to their characteristic ways of being, he is led rather naturally to follow the double similarity of signs to objects or to impressions, and of signs to each other. First, there are some inflections given as natural signs of pleasure, grief, surprise, fear, admiration, etc.; these inflections, which are like the cry of the soul, are soon applied to the objects themselves, which are apt to arouse the sentiments which they express, become the principal and general roots of their compound names and may determine a beginning of the classification of objects which have among them, if I may so express myself, the same relations of *affective similarity*. As to sonorous, noisy objects, they themselves dictate the names which are to portray them; another fertile source of similarity, which is found in all languages and moreover most frequently the more primitive they are the better they have preserved the primordial type of their origin.

In the second place, the number of the keys of the vocal instrument and consequently of the simple intonations of the human voice, is limited and determined. Their possible combinations are, doubtless, prodigiously extensive, since they are sufficient and more for all varieties of description through sounds, and for this innumerable multitude of words which compose different languages among which at the first glance no relation is perceived; but, in attending only to elementary tones and to their simplest combinations, it is clear that the principal imitative words will preserve at first among them the similarity which results from the constant repetition of the same elements, and must represent or imitate afterwards the similarities which nature follows in the productions of the same climate, in the uniform colors in which she is represented and the habitual impressions to which her pictures give rise.

The individual who creates a language will, therefore, not at first multiply the signs so much as the variety of the objects which he distinguishes would seem to require. He will follow the similarities more than the differences, and will be led to classify his signs and impressions by the same propensity which already brings the child to classify the objects which resemble each other, either first by generalizing individual names or by afterwards applying to them the names of number, etc. This method, which singularly abridges and facilitates the operation of naming as well as that of recalling, will therefore be one of the chief habits of the individual.

2. The similarity which rules in the principal system of vocal signs, must first influence the very material of language and secondarily the association of ideas which it determines.

If the same elementary tones are frequently reproduced, and if their combinations are subjected to uniform laws, the corresponding keys of the vocal instrument will acquire by the continual repetiton of the same exercise, a very great flexibility. Habit will fix these *animated strings* on one persisting tone; and the system of words will soon no longer revolve except upon itself, excluding every new element which would not be similar to it. It will be, therefore, here as with all movements, as with all the operations which are most frequently repeated. In proportion as habit makes us execute them with more ease and promptitude, it restrains our faculties and hinders them from being extended outside of the same circle.

It is well known with what difficulty (particularly at a certain age) the words of a foreign language are articulated; it may be contrasted only with the automatic facility with which the mother tongue is spoken.

Let us now suppose, therefore, that by the combined effects of similarity and habit, the individual is perfectly familiarised with the system of articulated signs which he has made for himself and let us see what will be the results of this extreme facility which he has for finding, recalling, and articulating names.

3. In the beginning, when it was a matter of observing an object, an impression, or an idea, it was necessary to look for the sign, to articulate it slowly and with an effort proportional to the inflexibility of the vocal organ and at the same time to attend to the object or idea and not to lose sight of them. This energy of a double attention, this simultaneous use of motor activity on two organs, could only favor the association and deepen the imprint of the image and the sign and at the same time prepare for the nicety of representation of the one and for the facility of recall of the other. But it might happen also that the difficulty of articulation had concentrated the attention too exclusively upon the sign and then the latter would remain isolated in the memory. Its recall would be no longer more than a simple movement. It would not give any hold on the image, which would be concealed from the gaze of thought. On the contrary, when language has become habitual, the rapidity with which words are presented and articulated, as of their own accord, leaves the motor activity inactive, does not develop the attention or makes it glide with equal lightness over the sign and over its idea. The first, therefore, will then escape recall as the other, representation, or both faculties will remain in their respective states of independence; the imagination will not be ruled by the signs, or the signs will be empty and without object.

When the individual, for example, on the one hand preoccupied with the vivacity and charm of the images, is on the other hand carried away by the familiarity of the associated terms, the faint degree of attention which he accords to the signs does not permit the images to be recalled; they will, therefore, have shone for a few instants only to disappear immediately like meteors, without its being possible to find any traces of them again; or if the activity of the brain, which produced them, should bring them back, the individual, not having connected his signs of recognition with them, would think that he saw them for the first time. He must, therefore, mistrust that extreme facility of language, for if he does not take care, habit tends through that very fact to bring him back to his original point of departure, to blind him to the source and number of his characteristic operations, finally to interrupt that close communication that he would want always to maintain with his thought. If he does not take care, the absence of all effort, in vocal movement, will put his attention to sleep and distract it even from the images, as *felt* articulation tended formerly to reflect it there. Then all the associations will err by a lack of weight; the series of words will succeed each other uselessly in the memory or drag ideas in their wake without any vestige remaining of any of them; or finally, the individual, mistaking the functions of his signs, no longer perceiving the activity that he exercises in recall, will end by confusing it with the passive exercise of the imagination and, letting himself go with the stream, will forget that he is endowed with a power to react on his thought and to modify himself. But, preoccupied with the effects which the great habit of language produces on us in our communications, we forget that a solitary person who would have created his signs and would only use them for himself, would be less exposed to such inconveniences. Besides, continual reflection would make him always watch the connections which unite his signs to his ideas, for fear that they would relax to the point of seeming isolated or that they would crowd together in such a way as to be merged—effects of habit equally pernicious, as we shall have opportunity to convince ourselves in what follows. Let us still linger on some other forms of the association of language, in order to come to the conclusions which we wish to deduce from all this.

4. We have so far supposed that the individual gave names only to objects or to images of his perceptions. But the power-

ful help that he draws from his signs, the advantages and progress which result from them, must bring him to extend them to all that he can feel, distinguish, or conceive in himself. It seems to him, in fact, that he appropriates, incorporates in some way with his thought, all that he retains there by a name: this name is like a frame, a work of his hands; it circumscribes the picture, makes it dearer to him, and takes away from it that veil of indifference, which habit spreads over familiar objects. Since he has experienced the power of the signs to recall and fix various impressions which escaped him, why would he not try particularly to submit to the same power those sensations, those affective modifications, which flee so quickly and which he would be so happy to retain and to revive at his will?

He has, therfore (and doubtless very early), some signs expressive of different sensations which he may experience in his organs and, in general, of pleasure, of well-being, and of voluptuousness; he has also some for grief, discomfort, etc. Every slightly different gradation of feeling may have a distinct name in his memory; but it is not enough to have a name, its association with the thing signified must be so fixed that it cannot be separated from it in recall, and that the very voluntary act, which is directly exercised on the sign, can make the image live again in the mind, or the faint impression in the organ; without that it remains only an empty sound, a simple movement. But, in order for an association to have been able first to be formed in that close manner and consequently to bring about such results, the motor activity, as we have already observed, must be equally and simultaneously spread over the two terms. The impression and the sign must have been included in one common (*active*) attention. But here the nature of things excludes this equality, this freedom of attention, and the same organic causes, which deprive the sensation of primitive voluntary signs, will hinder it from being regularly associated with signs artificially subsumed.

In fact, has the actual, affective modification a certain degree of vivacity? How can we freely think of or attend to the operation which must note it or circumscribe it? Is it weak or indifferent? It disappears and is lost in the very act which tends to fixate it. After the sensation has ceased to exist, certain accessory and in themselves perceptible circumstances may, it is true, awake the memory of it: will the individual, apprehending this more or less confused remembrance, give it a sign? But then will this not just augment the number of preexisting accessory circumstances, on which remembrance is already based, and fortify it by a new sign, a *free sign* in truth and one which will serve (like a monument that is visited at will) to testify that it has been modified on such and such an occasion and in such and such circumstances as it represents, but without power to awaken anything like the past modification, still less to reproduce the *idea*?

Nevertheless, it may happen that in certain physical conditions, the recall of the associated sign excites in the organs a kind of trembling, even produces on the whole system a sort of electrical effect; this is not yet an *idea* of sensation, but a very real, present affection on the renewal of which the sign will never have a direct and constant power.

The function of signs associated with feelings or any affective modifications, will therefore be either nothing or stimulative, and in this latter case, always variable and undertermined. It will then differ essentially from the *representative* function of which we spoke in the first place. Nevertheless, if the individual did not reflect, he would feel himself incessantly prompted to confuse them; habit would make him extend, without his perceiving it, the power of his first real associations to all that he would have been able, in the course of time, to invest with signs; and he would firmly think that he had ideas every time that he would find words in his memory. This illusion would particularly dominate thought, when the names would be connected with truly archetypal ideas, with purely imaginary concepts, with fantastic, mysterious beings, sources of fears or hopes, etc. But let us not anticipate what we must say elsewhere, and let us not push further a fiction which, in the main improbable, has none the less furnished us with results directly applicable to the fundamental habits of our language. Let us summarize them here in a few words and conclude.

1. That the articulated signs, associated secondarily with perceptions, replace the original movements, which have become insensible through their continual repetition, renew the activity of consciousness, lost or concealed as the result of habit, suit the impressions to the motor faculty of recall and make them pass from the domain of the imagination to that of memory.

2. That the extreme facility and rapidity of language tends to reduce to a blind mechanism all the operations for which it serves as basis, to obscure their source, to make their nature and number misconceived; that this effect of habit corresponds to the progressive diminishing of vocal effort or of the active determination, and hides from us the bonds which unite our signs to our ideas (as it conceals from us those which exist between the principal movements and determinations of touch, and visual impressions); that this is why we too frequently speak emptily while believing that we think, or why we think with the rapidity of speech without suspecting its necessity (as we do not believe in the necessity of the intervention of touch in the judgments of sight): effects the consequence of which we shall soon see.

3. That in all cases where it is a question of associating a sign with a perception, or with a predetermined image, it is always the fault of the individual, of his haste, of his weakness of habit, if the association is irregular or badly made and the recall without representative effect. But all his efforts at attention are useless or this voluntary attention is itself impossible, when he wishes to extend the power of his signs outside of the limits of representation; for nature, which has not given signs of recall to purely affective sensations or modifications, does not wish art to be more powerful than she.

4. In the association of signs and ideas, it is important, therefore, to distinguish the obstacles which may arise from

the nature of one or the other of the terms to be associated. The effort or the determination of the movement (*sign*) may have too much or too little intensity; the impression may be too faint or too affective: there is no regular association possible except in the equal and simultaneous development of the motor activity over the two terms, which presupposes that they are both equally submitted or appropriated. These results lead us actually to distinguish different functions of signs and as many parallel modes in the exercise of the faculty which consists, in general, of recalling them.

If signs are absolutely empty of ideas or separated from every representative effect, from whatever cause this isolation may arise, recall is only a simple repetition of movements. I shall call the faculty for it *mechanical memory*.

When the association is grounded exactly on the conditions of which we have spoken, and which alone may render it useful, the recall of the sign being accompanied or immediately followed by the clear appearance of a well circumscribed idea, I shall attribute it to *representative memory*.

If the sign expresses an affective modification, a feeling or even a fantastic image whatsoever, a vague, uncertain concept, which cannot be brought back to sense impressions (common source of every idea, of every real notion), and which, through that very fact, enjoys a more stimulative property, the recall of the sign, considered in this latter relation, will belong to *sensitive memory*.

These three faculties are only three modes of the application of the same motor activity which *recalls*. But they differ essentially, as much by the nature of the objects and, so to say, materials on which they are exercised as by the very remarkable habits which their repeated exercise may cause to be contracted in the organ of thought; that is what I propose to investigate in the following chapters.

CHAPTER II

The Exercise and Habits of Mechanical Memory

Articulated sounds or tones, considered by themselves and abstracted from all actual representative value, are only the simple products of motor activity. If they differ from other voluntary *movements*, in the strict sense of the term, it is because the latter are not made known to consciousness except through this particular impression of *effort*, which is always proportional to the resistance or the inertia of the organs; while the sound is doubly sensible to the individual who voluntarily emits it, both by this same effort and by the perception of it that hearing receives.

To retain, to recall sounds, to exercise mechanical memory, is, therefore, only to retain and repeat a series of movements; furthermore, this memory of words is the first to be exercised. It is the one of our faculties the cultivation of which is the simplest, the surest, the most extended in its results. Its growth is as sensible and seems to follow the same laws as that of the muscular powers.

The habits of this active faculty, the manner in which they are contracted, the effects which they produce, bear the imprint of the most perfect mechanism, and indicate their origin themselves. It is this of which we are going to judge, in applying to the subject before us what we have said in general of the repetition of our movements.

1. Given a series of words to learn, as they say, *by heart* or to recite in a definite and determined order; let these terms be intelligible and represent ideas connected with each other or not, it matters little enough to the present purpose; for it would be equally necessary to concentrate all our attention on the material of the sounds or characters. Otherwise, we would

retain indeed the sense of such and such a phrase, of such and such a discourse, but by the very one which would be adapted to the ideas, it would frequently become impossible to state them precisely in the same terms or in the same order and we would thus fall short of the proposed end. It is, therefore, exclusively to the successive association of certain vocal movements that it is important to attend. For that, it is at first necessary to insist upon each articulation, to use a certain degree of effort, to impress in a word upon the organ principally concerned the determinations which must facilitate its activity. In repeating the same exercise many times, the vocal instrument rises little by little to a persisting tone. The attention or the use of forces necessary in the beginning to execute each particular movement progressively diminishes; soon the animated spring will act by itself at the faintest impulsion. Recall, being simply exercised on the first term, all the others will proceed to arrange themselves in line in their order without being called, without its being even possible to avert them. This is indeed the promptitude, nimbleness, automatism of habitual movements.

In articulating habitual formulas, thought is therefore lazy or distracted, and the mechanism only goes the better for it. A superfluous attention would check its activity, as a function too great and disproportionate to the resistance stiffens the muscles and hinders their activity.

The fixity which vocal determinations have acquired, the almost complete and actual independence which they have of the will which formed them in the beginning, makes clear to us why it is so difficult to insert new terms, to change the order, the speed of succession; the measure, the accent, the raising or lowering of the voice on certain syllables, etc., when all that is changed into mechanism by long and frequent repetition. Thus is justified the title which we have given to this kind of Memory.

2. The one who has to-day made such and such a number of movements will tomorrow be capable of making a greater, and

so forth.   As the one who carried the newly-born calf every day
will end by carrying the cow, in the same way the one who has
learned by heart ten lines in one day, can learn twelve of them
the next day, etc.; and one is praised for this material progress
which is, so to say, measured by lengths.   It is not, however, in
this manner that the true progress of intelligence is measured.
It is not thus, advancing, so to say, in a same straight line,
that thinking power is developed.   Its delicate springs must
be handled with a little more care and caution; they are moreover subject to more disturbances and anomalies in their activity.

Nevertheless, however generally extended are these mechanical forces, habit itself fixes and circumscribes them within certain limits.   Upon general tendencies or upon the particular
bent which it has impressed upon our motor activity always
depend the degrees of ease or difficulty, trouble or attraction which we experience, when we try to pass from one kind
or one series of movements, acts, or impressions to a new series.
Similarity alone may in this case procure us some help, some
resting-places, make the transition easy and the change agreeable.

The similarity of sounds and words, like that of every kind of
impressions, ideas, etc., may be based only on their partial
identity, on the frequent reproduction of like elements which
compose them.   If there are many of these elements common
to two terms or two series, the organ preoccupied with one is
quite disposed already to lend itself to the other.   It is at once
change and constancy, variety and uniformity; hence the facility and attraction.   On the contrary, if it is necessary to pass
from one familiar series to another which is opposed to it or
which does not contain any common element, it is necessary
to do violence to all our habits; hence the difficulties and
trouble.   When we are accustomed, for example, only to recite
verses, we generally learn prose with more or less difficulty;
and generally, we have much more tendency to retain poetry.
The similar terminations, the periodic recurrence of the same

syllables, especially the rhythm, the metre, are so many similitudes, which give wings to memory; the ear, struck as if by a series of even and repeated beats at equal intervals, transmits those *isochronal* vibrations to the motor center, which, naturally disposed to admit them, there coördinates its own activity and easily contracts the habit of reproducing them with particular regularity and precision.

Although the rhythm of poetry is only a result of the choice and arrangement of words, it is worthy of note that it is frequently retained independently of those words, is transformed into habits before they are, and thus becomes the principal cause of memory (*numeros memini si verba tenerem.* Virgil's Eclogues). The rhythm is to the habits of the ear, what symmetry is to those of the eye.

3. The means which we have just indicated, while they extend and facilitate the exercise of mechanical memory, may also furnish powerful aids to the representative faculty; the analogy which rules even in the material forms of the signs favors equally, as is well known, the nicety of representation of the ideas with which they are associated. But it is the circumstances which are exclusively allied to the mechanism with which we are here occupied and which are apt to change it into a ruling habit.

These circumstances may, moreover, be drawn from the particular character of the usual signs; in the second place, from the manner in which these signs have first entered the memory; and from the functions which they continue to fulfil there when repeated.

A. Spoken or written words may have a character adapted to fixing or concentrating the attention upon them, instead of reflecting it back upon the ideas: for example, if their articulation was at first very difficult; if their elements drawn from the most disagreeable notes of the vocal instrument are gathered together without a similarity present to consciousness in long and involved expressions. To learn to speak, to remember only the words of our own language would be a large undertaking and as we would have contracted the habit of it only by dint of work and time, we would still continue, through habit, to attend more to signs than to things, we would incessantly feed the mechanical memory, its products would always be creditable and important and the sciences of words would be in esteem.

On the contrary, soft, brilliant, sonorous articulations are soon appropriated by the vocal organ, the flexible mobility of which they maintain. But they flatter the ear so agreeably, that they are remembered for themselves; they are like a series of melodious tones which make the *motif* of the composer forgotten. The sensibility of hearing is thus exercised, but thought remains lazy and is habituated to inactivity.

It is thus that mechanical memory may be adjusted to two extremes. Its habits are also strengthened by the use of *arbitrary* signs, after they have lost the traces of their origin and after their first conscious impress is erased. The conventions which determine their value are too frequently vague, they are ignored or forgotten. A certain amount of work is always necessary in order to get back to them and it is so easy to remember the words, to run rapidly through the series of them. A written language (for example, like that of the Chinese) forces one to think in reading, while our writing leads us only to articulated speech, which in itself too frequently leads us to nothing.

B. The greater part of the words which we have learned in our childhood have at first been only simple habits of the ear and the voice. Mechanical memory has been almost entirely alone in forming our first vocabulary (I mean one which first extended beyond our needs and the objects which immediately strike our senses). An unintelligent education has taken possession of these formless materials which chance or circumstances have presented and has built upon them. We already could articulate enough senseless words, and did our secondary education frequently have any other object than to increase and extend this first store? Is it not almost always with meaningless words that we learn to read, write, translate, recite, etc.? What food for the young intelligence! Doubtless, it would have been fortunate for almost every one of us, if we had been deaf-mutes until the age of reason and if we had had Sicard's for instructors; we would not have known the yoke of mechanical habits of memory nor this triple wall of senseless terms from which it has afterwards been so difficult to free ourselves.

The effects which result from the exclusive exercise of mechanical memory are easy to perceive and too continual experience renders them sufficiently clear. The increasing rapidity of articulated terms most frequently hinders every deliberate return to ideas, which remain of no force or vague and indetermined. Facility degenerates into automatism, excludes every effort at attention. Thought languishes, its powers are lost, its organ becomes incapable of fulfilling its real functions. Everything, so to say, happens outside of it. Nothing happens or persists in its inmost substance, nothing proceeds from its depths. As in those *athletic* temperaments (if I may use here a comparison which may be established up to a certain point) where the principle of life is concentrated in the muscles, increases their volume and mass and extends the *material operations of force* only at the expense of the more elevated functions; intelligence, here stifled by an objectless activity, grows only superficially, by swelling, and always lacks true energy, which has its source in a sensibility properly tempered by force.

CHAPTER III

The Exercise and Habits of Sensitive Memory

The gradation which separates mechanical memory from sensitive memory is, in certain cases, rather difficult to grasp. It is like the transition from night, when one sees nothing, to the faint and uncertain light of dawn, which misleads the sight among shadows and phantoms.

From the recall of a word quite empty of ideas to the recall of another word, accompanied by a *something* which is not an *idea*, but which is something more than a sound or a simple movement, the difference must be frequently insensible, particularly if this *something* disappears in the rapidity of articulation and leaves no more traces in thought than the breath escaped from the lips.

Mechanical memory revolves in the uniform sphere of articulated movements. Its exercise is simple. Its materials are almost all of the same nature, its habits constant, easy to recognize and indicate.

But from the vague extreme which borders upon nothingness to those energetic, impetuous feelings, which such and such words (although equally devoid of representation) have acquired the power to excite, the distance appears great; the gradations have greatly multiplied, the terms are singularly varied and heterogeneous. In the extreme variety of those terms and their sensory products, we shall principally apply ourselves to those which may best reveal to us the character of the faculty which they nourish. But first it is necessary to go back again to the primary associations of language, in order to seek there the causes which give the signs now such a changeable and uncertain meaning, now such an energetic and constant stimulative power. Hence will be easily deduced the different habits which must arise from the continual usage and repetition of signs of this kind.

Many of our terms were first designed to express sensations or affective modifications, desires, needs, feelings. That is what a primitive instinct brings us to manifest involuntarily and we afterwards lay hold of conventional signs which may put means at our disposal, with so much the more promptitude and facility, as they are almost merged with the movements or activities which nature alone had previously employed for the same end.

Our first language is, therefore, necessarily that of *sensations*. But, however so little we continue to follow it and adopt it through choice, its use may produce habits as sinister for the development of intelligence as its effectiveness as a *guide-post* had at first been useful and necessary for the conservation and maintenance of physical life.

The language of sensations and generally of feeling cannot be *representative* (as we have seen). It does not permit the exact impartiality of analysis, has besides no need of precision in order to be *nearly* understood, is even very well suited to vagueness and indetermination, and sometimes obtains from them its greatest results. In short, it is not within human power to give it any fixity; every rule, every constant modulation escapes it. And how, in fact, would the sign keep some fixed value, when the thing expressed incessantly varies? Let us suppose, for example, that a name is applied to an odor, a flavor, any simple *sensation* whatsoever (freed, if it is possible, from all that is not itself), this modification, agreeable as a novelty, becomes indifferent or displeasing through habit. It is then no longer the same but, nevertheless, it keeps the same name. An old man will use the same terms to express the feelings and pleasures which he relished when his organs were in their prime. Can one imagine that the signs have always the same meaning for him? It is then through a very illusory judgment, through a profound habit, the effects of which we shall indicate elsewhere, that we transfer the identity of the sign and the fixity of the *perceptible* associated circumstances to the modification which no longer exists.

If we were, therefore, limited to speaking of what we have *felt*, our expressions would always be either nearly empty or at least very vague, indefinite and indefinable. Continual repetition of the same language would produce in us a habit of irresolution or of illusions of many kinds, and in that way would swallow up every capacity, every *truth* of representation, all the real energy of thought.

Such would be the general effects of the slack and uncertain language of sensations. But the exercise of the sensitive memory is further based on terms which have a singular power of stimulating different signs of *archetypal* ideas, which acquire in thought a consistency frequently equal to that of real objects and always a greater power. The energy of these effects continually grows through the repetition or the free recall of the same articulated sounds. Thence arise the most deep-seated, obstinate habits, those the causes of which it would be most important to know in order to avert and moderate their terrible influence.

Here is presented under another aspect the same question which we have already proposed (in Chapter IV of the preceding section).

How does it happen that certain sentiments, far from fading through the ordinary effect of habit, acquire on the contrary an increasing force and vivacity, through the frequent recall of the associated signs which express them? . . . . All the results which the first has furnished us with may be applied to the present question; for the basis of the question is indeed the same; it is composed of like elements. But here the persistency of habits increases still more, the effects are extended and complicated both by the intervention of *free* signs which the individual may reproduce at any instant, and by which he is himself inspired, and by the particular fantastic ideas which are allied to the use of these signs and would not exist without them; in short, through the different combinations which they establish and determine, the comparisons and judgments which they motivate.   It is in these new relations that we shall examine the materials and the habits of sensory memory.

II. The sensitive and active being is instinctively an imitator. The movements, gestures, accent, tone, all the external manifestations of his environment, make an impression on him early and attract his attention; he is trained to imitate, to repeat all that he sees done and his motor organs acquire many activities, long indeed before his thought is capable of apprehending their purpose or of fathoming their motives.

Those activities, those external signs which the child imitates, are connected (in the minds of those who serve him as models) with feelings; these feelings are perhaps connected with some ideas, and the feelings as well as the ideas with some articulated sounds which at the same time express both. The child at first apprehends the movements and the word through the same principle of imitation; soon undoubtedly by another sympathetic effect, he will experience the feeling; but the idea (if it exists), being always the most difficult, the furtherest removed, and the least interesting to know, will only come late and will perhaps always remain fluctuating and uncertain.

Let one frequently, for example, stimulate the ears of a child with certain terms corresponding to any archetypal ideas whatever. Let him unite to this articulation some signs or movements of the body and the face, which express veneration, respect, admiration or fright, fear, horror, scorn, etc. The child surely does not connect distinct ideas with all that. But he repeats and firmly remembers the words, gestures, attitudes which will soon lead him to experience some shades of the feelings which they express and that in proportion to the development of his sensibility, which these very circumstances may render more precocious.

When through the effect of assiduous repetition, these sounds, movements and feelings are closely associated together, whatever word happens then to strike the ear or to be presented to memory determines, as if through an involuntary and mechanical force, the same activity in the motor organs and the accustomed excitation in the sensible system. Thus it is that repeated examples and old habits lead the greater part of mankind to admire, to be enraptured, to shudder, to tremble, to be indignant, in short to fly into all sorts of passions, at *words* which are the most insignificant, the vaguest and the emptiest of ideas, and which through the very violence of the feelings which they excite, are condemned to remain always in the most complete indetermination.

If the terms thus learned and ranked among the primary materials of sensitive memory, are going to refer to invisible beings, judged or supposed to exist in the profundities of time and space, the imagination soon takes possession of them as of its own food and hastens to tint them with some colors and to invest them with some forms; this more or less confused representation fortifies the judgment of *real existence* and gives a reason for fear or hope. From that time, the images take a new predominance; the judgment which makes them real receives from them a new force. All the determinations are deepened by their duration and by the repetition of the same signs and the same causes which have given rise to them. Thus one *believes* at first in what one imagines. One's *belief* is proportional to what one feels, to what one likes to *feel* (even to fear). When one has ceased to imagine, one still believes in the same *words* through habit and because one no longer remembers the first and *material* causes of his belief.

Thus it is that children, and many grown-up children, have learned to believe firmly in the existence of sorcerers, ghosts, fairies, spirits, Tartarus, the Elysian Fields, etc. When associations of this nature, in which the imagination and the feeling involve judgment or faith, have been cemented by long-standing habit, it is then that the words which have established them through lengthy repetition, seem endowed with a supernatural magic power; their articulation, their recall, convulse the whole system, as if by an electric shock. How then can these terms henceforth bear cold and deliberate examination, the calm and severe glance of reason? Will it question the foundations of a blind belief? But it stops involuntarily before those nominal titles which their old age consecrates. It trembles and is humiliated. Will it weigh in its balance a host of confused notions which float at the will of the habits, of the prepossessions and the blind prejudices of childhood? But these terms, in striking the ear or the eye, still make some old sensitive cord vibrate and the philosopher becomes again a child. In vain he struggles against this terrible power. In vain he believes that he is freed from its bonds and that he penetrates with all the freedom and profundity of reflection to the pure regions of truth; the first products of the sensory memory creep among the elements of a wise analysis perhaps without being perceived; and the work constructed with those heterogeneous materials will be comparable to those old repaired edifices, where the attentive eye once more unravels the traces of singular gothic forms which all the labours and talents of the architect have not been entirely able to erase. Such is the power of early habits!

III. If we again attribute to sensory memory every term which, deprived of any representative capacity whatsoever, nevertheless excites some more or less energetic and more or less obscure or confused feelings, we shall find a vast field open to the exercise and habits of this faculty in the abstractions, the reveries, the hypotheses of philosophers (or of those who have for a long time usurped this title), and especially in the illusory comparisons on which they have often constructed vain systems.

When, transferring to chimerical concepts some of the properties and consequently the very names of familiar objects, they pervert the value of the signs and purposely make them at first pass over from the natural and appropriate sense to the abstract and imagined; then, from the very habit of considering them under this new aspect they forget or fail to recognize their early origin. When, by dint of contemplating the sensible in the abstract, they end by identifying or confusing them; when in short their imagination, put into activity by the vagueness, the uncertainty, and the double meaning of terms, throws a deceitful glow upon shadows and imprints upon them the color and consistency of reality; do they do anything but extend the domain of sensory memory, increase (through *mixed* expressions, through simple names become mysterious) the number of its materials, in short, do they do anything but strengthen habits of which the duration and repute of their systems would suffice to show all the tenacity?

The systematic visions of philosophers, the seductive illusions of poets, the needs of the imagination and, above all, this power of the first signs of habit which leads us to judge of identity by the most imperfect analogies (see Chapter III, first part, first article), all have contributed to alter the title of the (at first) representative terms, to make them pass insensibly and by one of the very effects of habit from the literal to the figurative, from the concrete to the abstract, from the imitative to the arbitrary: thence must have resulted in ordinary intercourse, various abuses of language almost like those which have served as a foundation for the abstract systems of philosophers.

When the figurative sense has become literal through the repeated use that has been made of it, the first sensible imprint being absolutely erased, the sign has no longer exercised any but an arbitrary function and must have frequently degenerated into a pure mechanism, as we have observed in the preceding chapter. But before reaching this state, there has doubtless frequently happened what happens to ourselves when we voluntarily and perhaps unnecessarily transfer the name of a sensible object to an abstract idea. The metaphoric expression seems to enlighten us then with a double light, one direct, the other reflected. But these two kinds of rays may cross each other in thought, which being thus enlightened by a false light, sees nothing distinct and remains undecided or, perceiving only delusive appearances, takes a wrong direction and leaves reality in order to follow shadows. This uncertainty, these illusions, these surprises, which are so fitted to arouse our feelings, similarly weaken the faculty of representation. Repeated and immoderate use of figures, gradually increasing the number of vague and indefinite expressions, will thus fortify the habits of sensory memory and render them predominant.

In general, the more a language abandons tropes of every kind, allegories, metaphors, inversions, etc., the more will the signs fulfil a stimulative function and the more will their constant use favor the exercise of the faculty of which we speak. Abstract systems, systematised visions of all kinds arise and reproduce their kind there as in their natural element; this will be the favorite language of the seducers and enemies of human reason. It will be able to furnish weapons to some and talismans to others.

The repetition of signs exclusively adapted to excite feeling (and it seems that they may produce this effect in many ways) succeeds in modifying the organ of thought to a certain degree, as the use of artificial stimulants modifies and adjusts the internal organs—the centers of sensibility. Thought is likewise linked to habitual springs of excitation, demands them back again, incessantly calls for them, can no longer do without them nor free itself from them, and nevertheless it is disgusted with all the essentially good foods and loses, if one may thus express it, the faculty of digesting them. Thus we see those men accustomed to feed upon illusions repulse obstinately all the products of enlightened reason, as elements foreign to their natures.

To express habits, or constant tendencies of thought, which would arise from the repeated exercise of mechanical memory, we took for the object of comparison that kind of temperament in which the motor activities dominate and absorb the sensory activities; we now relate habits, the formation and general effects of which we have just indicated, to that other temperament, in which sensibility predominates over activity. Although these tendencies appear opposed to each other, they nevertheless have for common results the abduction of the will, the incapacity for attention and reflection, the inertia of the representative faculty.   Let us see how this last faculty may arise and be strengthened by the repetition of means adapted to restoring and maintaining the equilibrium of forces.

CHAPTER IV

THE EXERCISE AND HABITS OF REPRESENTATIVE MEMORY; INFORMATION CONCERNING THE PROPER WAYS OF FORMING THESE HABITS

Memory or recall of signs, memory or representation of forms and figures, that is perhaps to what will be reduced, in the last analysis, all the operations, all the real and consistent products of what we have called human intelligence.

Signs can only have representative value through the ideas with which they are associated. Ideas (taking this word in its proper and direct meaning) can only be images or copies of perceptions and there is real perception only of forms, figures and sounds (see the Introduction). All the rest fly like shadows. *"Par levibus ventis volucrique simillima somno."*

Our perceptions, ideas, and signs are derived from the same source and belong to the same class of *active* impressions. We may then, in this connection, consider them as homogeneous elements; and, indeed, the facility with which these elements become united, the ever uniform persistance, duration, and clearness which their compounds enjoy, can depend only on their nature, their intrinsic properties. Art may indeed bring them together, put them into close contact, but does not determine the affinity, the force of aggregation which is inherent in them.

The articulated sign and the visible or tangible object, for example, with which this sign is connected, are two equally distinct, equally fixed and free perceptions. Motor activity may be divided between these two terms, include them in the same act without there being sensory disturbance which arrests or diverts its manifestation. The same exercise may be continued or repeated, according to the will of the individual.

172

The principal conditions of a close and lasting association are thus perfectly satisfied (see Chapter I, second section). Henceforth the presence of the object will determine the recall of the sign, and this recall will provoke the appearance of the image. The function is common and reciprocal. Recall is facilitated by the familiarity of perception, and representation by the frequency of voluntary recall. Memory resting here equally upon the sign which leads to the idea and upon the object which leads back to the sign, will thus have a double source. Its habits will also acquire double persistency. Names will not be empty and will not leave in thought any cloud which may not be promptly dissipated by new experiences. In short (and this inestimable advantage is exclusively connected with the class of our perceptible impressions) the fixity of the image corresponds to that of the free articulated sign or the permanence of the sign written or drawn as the constant value of this sign rests in its turn on the invariability of the object that it represents; there are no illusions, delusions or mechanical habits there. Fixed by these admirable instruments, which necessity or genius invented and the use of which habit has facilitated, the latter produces constancy in thought, as nature maintains it externally. Happy would we be if all the materials of our knowledge, all the elements of our constructions were always as solid and unalterable!

The varied needs of the social and infinitely perfectible being, the characteristic activity of thought, the development and extension, which the constant and continually repeated use of the linguistic signs procures for these needs and this activity, soon draw the individual outside of the too narrow circle of perceptions, images, and signs directly associated with their objects. Departing from these elements as fixed points, he submits them to new operations, elaborates, combines, groups, and separates them in an infinity of ways. What could put limits to his power?

He has *power* n himself, *raw material* in the signs, and he creates, or rather he orders, he forms the new world of his ideas with materials extracted from the real world. While living in one, he must then never forget the other; he must look there and always be able to find there again the number, quality, and place of the elements which he has drawn from it. But, it is representative memory which alone can furnish those indications. It is on it that the freedom of communication between the two worlds depends and the passage which it furnishes is always so much the more prompt and sure the more frequently it has been summoned to visit and verify in detail the parts of the ideal compound, or the less these parts themselves are falsified or disguised, in short the closer to their sensible originals.

To appreciate the nature of the functions of representative memory, in the use of these terms or secondary compounds, to judge of the facility with which it may fulfil these functions and to recognize the habits which it contracts through the repetition of these different exercises, it will now be proper to examine (or at least to indicate here rapidly) what are, in the principal classes of our compound ideas, the particular characteristics which adapt them more to the faculty of which we speak.

First, let us rid this name of *idea* of all that is related to the exercise of feeling, all that belongs to the stimulative function of the sign. If this last is not an *empty sound*, it will be able to express only a representable object or one susceptible of being restored to clear representations of the senses (by a more or less long chain of operations of analysis, etc.).

1. Let us take for the first example the terms for moral notions, which offer us the double property of being *sensory*, which we pointed out in the preceding chapter, and *representative*, with which we are now occupied.

These terms, as is well known, include under them ideas of different kinds, which admit various sorts of elements themselves compound, etc.; in such a way that it is always more or less difficult to restore them to simple and primitive perceptions of the senses. Nevertheless, as the real and principal foundation of these ideas can never be drawn except from perceptions themselves, combined and transformed in different ways, there is no doubt that memory can contract the habit of representing them exactly with the aid of their signs; and with so much the more clearness, promptitude, and ease, as the same combinations have been more carefully executed, more frequently repeated and above all as the examples which have determined their formation have been more frequently reproduced externally.   These examples, in fact, although composed of a very great number of details, are circumscribed in one and the same picture and become the object of a single or of many rapidly succeeding acts of representative memory.

This is why we represent, with the quickness of speech, what composes, generally, the *material* of different actions or circumstances, which we are accustomed to connect with such and such a term in ethics.   (There are, moreover, few *virtues* or *vices* which cannot be represented by sensible images; and morality too is susceptible of being put into pictures; this is perhaps the best way of attaining its end.)   But the terms under discussion here are not only destined to represent the material of actions with their *perceptible* circumstances, they further indicate *relations* of many kinds, and most of the relations are of such a nature that they must not and cannot be *measured* (as all that is called, with most reason, by the name of relation), but indeed must be *felt*. Such is, for example, the relation of a son to his father, in the word parricide; that of obligation to one's benefactor, in the word ingratitude, etc.

It is necessary to distinguish the picture or clear representation, which our minds produce from moral actions and circumstances connected with a sign, from the feeling with which we may be affected through the recall of the sign or through the representation of the picture.   These two last acts, depending on the habits of memory or imagination, may acquire their constancy and fixity.   But feeling is very apt to vary in each individual (and often in the same one at different times), according to the physical conditions, the temperature, the degree of moral development, which is proportional to that of a sensibility more or less trained, in short according to the early education and the acquired experience of the virtues and evils of life, an experience which alone can make these virtues and evils conceived or shared and determine our sympathy or our aversion for them.   Sometimes even (as we have already seen) this feeling, not being founded on any representation or any idea, is connected only with the articulated sound, which acquires from an early habit of imitation the power of exciting it.   Finally, it is always possible to define the *idea*: previous combinations or analyses frequently repeated, may facilitate for thought the means of retaining them and of including their numerous elements.   But feeling because of its very nature escapes the power of those artificial means, which are foreign to it and can no more capture it than give it birth.

It is with mental beauty as with physical beauty.   One may learn to apprehend and to judge of a picture as a whole through an easy and ready application of the rules of art, to which one is accustomed; but one does not learn in the same way to *feel* beauties keenly.

Perhaps one could succeed in making an Asiatic, for example, conceive the real ideas which we can attach to the terms *patriotism, honor*, etc.; but it would be quite as difficult to instil in him the feelings of them as to make him participate in the physical and sensual tastes suited to our climates and to the principal habits of our senses.

Let us conclude that the terms of moral notions, which Locke named *mixed modes*, have generally two functions, one relative to the habits of representative memory; the other to habits or conditions of sensitivity.   We have seen how these latter may be formed (preceding chapter).   The others are only perceptions or images, simultaneously associated with each other and with a sign; this association is more difficult, and requires a more considerable number of repetitions, in proportion as the elements of the picture are more numerous, more varied, more heterogeneous and above all more fleeting, since they are not connected with any external and fixed model.   Let us add

further that the feeling excited by the recall of the sign frequently troubles and obscures the distinctness of representation.

2. Representative memory further fulfils the most important
and necessary functions in the regular formation as well as in
the recall of the terms of our different abstract and general
and mixed complex ideas of every kind.   First in their formation, it is representative memory which furnishes, comform-
ably to its acquired habits, the signs and the images, or elementary sensible ideas, of objects perceived simultaneously or at
different times; the individual then contemplates in those
compared copies, what he had not perceived in the models;
he establishes in his ideal world an order, which, transferred
again to the external world, extends and singularly facilitates
his knowledge of it.   It is thus that he arranges and orders his
ideas beside one another according to their diverse similarities
or abstracts their common properties and forms new groups
representative of those properties; gives to each group a particular sign which thus becomes the common designation
of a smaller or greater number of individuals and classifies them
under those labels of genus, class, species, etc., as in so many
pigeons-holes where it is always easy to find them again.

Terms formed in this way, on the returns of the memory,
are again entrusted to its depository.   It alone can represent
them exactly, with the real value which has been given them.
Its habitual intervention, its fidelity can alone prevent errors,
illusions, and self-willed habits, which are so frequently
connected with the vague and mechanical use of like terms.
But let us abridge details which would take us too far from our
goal.   Let us take at random the sign of an abstract or complex
idea, of any sort whatsoever.   If it is not a sound empty of
meaning or a simple habit of the ear, what could be its function
if not to recall a certain determinate number of sensible qualities, which the feeble sight of our intelligence, not being able to
embrace in one glance, will apprehend or perceive in detail, in
the intermediary signs or ideas which are grouped to form

this structure, or indeed to lead us back and determine us to survey again in an inverse order the series of operations and comparisons which we executed on the direct representations of the senses or of the memory, before reaching the abstract term which is in question?   In all cases, to recall a bundle or a series of images through the associated signs which determine and circumscribe them is to exercise *representative memory*.

When the individual himself has formed his ideas, that is, carried out at first with the necessary care and attention, then frequently repeated in the same manner the operations which they presuppose; when in short he has firmly attached to the first sensible ring the thread which must direct him, he can rush boldly into the ethereal regions of the abstract world; his faithful memory will lead him back to the point of departure with all the assurance and readiness of its fortunate habits. Aside from these conditions, it is the emptiness and vagueness of imaginary space, it is nothingness.

3. What makes the functions of representative memory so difficult, so uncertain and so frequently invalid in the operations which have for their object to form or to resolve abstract or mixed complex terms, is particularly the heterogeneity which reigns among the elements combined or to be combined, among the ideas or sensible qualities, primarily separated or abstracted from different compared perceptions, then reunited under a single sign.   Among these qualities, if there are any which correspond to purely affective modifications, they will be unrepresentable and will necessarily carry over their indeterminableness into the artificial compounds of which they form a part. Moreover, in supposing them to be suited to the perceptive and representative faculties, they are not all equally so and do not at all permit the same distinctness.   In short, although there is a sort of natural affinity between our perceptions in the strict sense of the term, it nevertheless cannot be doubted that more time and habit are necessary to associate the impressions which belong to separate senses than those which are as a whole directed to the same organ.

But if there is a system of ideas which takes its source in a single class of impressions, or even in a same fundamental perception which is eminently and always equally distinct; if this perception does nothing but be transformed, repeated, added to itself to produce an infinite variety of modes and combinations; if the real similarity and identity which exist among these modes and combinations determine in the conventional signs which express them, an analogy and an identity such that the operations, which have fixed the value of the first terms, afterwards do nothing but repeat each other, following constant laws, in order to produce the highest combinations, in such a way that one could always mount and descend with equal ease and by the same continuous series, from the base to the top and from the top to the base; finally, if this precious similarity is represented and delineated to the eye in a permanent manner and strikes the ear in a series of periodically equal word-endings, etc., we shall find in these conditions as many motive powers suited to the action and habits of representative memory.

A. Our ideas of simple modes have their common origin in activity or in the impression of resistance, the fundamental basis of every perception and every idea. This primary impression, which in part communicates to all the others its distinctness and its fixedness, is itself obscured in combination. But if we can succeed in isolating it and freeing it from every mixture, it regains its perspicuity and is presented clearly to the understanding which is apprehending and contemplating it.

The resistance is repeated and is incessantly reproduced in everything that we handle and even, although more obscurely, in what we see, in every step, in every motion that we make beyond ourselves. If we take away every other sensible property, in order to consider only resisting objects or those capable of resisting our efforts, they will only be numerical unities (and does not the idea of unity as a matter of fact take its origin in an impression or the memory of an *indivisible* impression of resistance?).   Let us give a sign to the unity thus conceived. This sign suddenly acquires the greatest generality, since it is applied to everything that separately resists or that is *one*; and it, nevertheless, keeps its clearness and its perfect determinateness.

Let us now bring together or consider simultaneously two objects, *one* and *one*, or 1 and 1, and let us express this group by a new sign two or 2; let us again add another *one* and let us designate by the articulation or the character *three* or 3 the group of 2 + 1 ... and so on up to five or six.

The simplicity of the relation which we shall consider permits us to include or to represent simultaneously all those *ones*.   Our first signs will thus be representative; but they will cease to be so as soon as we make them express higher groups.

What do we do then?   Stopping at the last representative sign, we blend, or imagine blended in a single one, the unities it expresses.

We thus advance, repeating the same operations, always stopping at the number at which the representation ceases, in order to make a unity of a higher order, which will be denoted by a sign indicative of this order and analogous to that of a simple unity, etc.   This is how we can attain the highest combinations without losing sight of the direct knowledge which enlightened us in the lowest.

The signs which represent each group of units are generally like that of the first unit; they express only the repetition of a constant simple property which is found everywhere, in all the objects which are offered to the senses distinctly and separately, whatever be in other respects their nature and dissimilarity.   We shall thus have occasion at each moment to repeat and apply the names of numbers, and by dint of applying them to everything, we shall no longer apply them to anything; they will be detached from resisting objects and will subsist in the memory detachedly.   It is then that the signs, having passed from the concrete to the abstract, truly cease to be representative.   All turns upon the material of the characters which are directed to the eye or the ear.   The perfect analogy which the nature of the subject has permitted us to establish between those characters and their different combinations, this continual repetition of a few terms, this uniform circle of operations and formulas, are immediately adapted to mechanical memory. This faculty may then direct calculations with the assurance, readiness and automatism of habits; and unless one takes care, it tends to obscure the origin of the primary ideas of numbers, to hide the true foundation of the operations, in short to destroy every faculty of reflection.   In fact, how should the calculator acting by routine suspect any mystery in those operations which he practices blindly and with so much facility? It is not for him, it is not even always for the mathematician preoccupied with results and perhaps also partly blinded by habit, that it is reserved to know the niceties of the language of computation, to penetrate to its roots, and to discover the metaphysics, profound in its very simplicity, which presided at its formation.

Such are the advantages inherent in the nature of the ideas of simple modes, but also the inconveniences which may result from the habitual use of their terms.   These ideas are the clearest, the best suited to our representative faculty, the most susceptible of exact determination.   But, because their object is abstract, the idea is immediately merged with the sign (and habit itself tends to identify them more completely). Since everything is related to signs, mechanical memory often finds in them a food; and as the analogy which holds between them frequently restores the same operations, which the formulas, learned or remembered beforehand, apply almost in the same manner to all cases, the continual use of the same methods, the same formulas, possibly degenerating into a sort of automatism, will no longer exercise the activity of thought and will let its powers languish or be lost.

B. Of all our ideas of simple modes, those which are related to *space* or to the uniform properties of this plane solid, which we incessantly measure by our progressive movement, are always the most clearly circumscribed in our memory, the most amenable to representation, the least subject to being obscured in the uncertainty of signs or the mechanism of operations of which they are the object.

The ideas of *number* and *time* are acquired only by abstraction. All the knowledge and reality that they can retain in our thought, depend upon the signs which express them. The idea of space presupposes only our movement and is inseparable from it. Without numerical signs, there are only simple unities or impressions which succeed each other irregularly and without uniformity: without artificial signs, there is still a measured imagined space, representable to the senses and to memory by fixed points of division, *marks*, notes taken and kept in nature itself.

Divisions and numerical classifications are nothing without the operation which recalls the conventional value of the terms which express them. Divisions of duration have nothing fixed outside of space. But those of space itself are actual, *permanent:* they strike the senses and are always exactly verifiable, through the coöperation of the two principal organs of perception to which they are addressed, namely, touch and sight. If abstract ideas of other simple modes are compared with the sensible abstractions of imagined space, it will be seen how the latter are highly adapted to the exercise of representative memory and made in order to develop its best habits.

In separating extension from the other qualities of the object, it is delineated and represented to the eye; in contemplating these images we do not depart from the sensible world. It seems, on the contrary, that we have only succeeded in taking away the veil which dimmed the sight in order to facilitate a more distinct perception.

The relations of figures may be apprehended and perceived with sufficient exactitude by sight alone, and in training ourselves to make these comparisons, sense becomes more exact and precise, and thought more correct.

It is always on perceptions or ideas themselves that it is a question of acting and not at all on the signs alone.   There are no formulas all prepared, terms evaluated in advance in such matters.   All that is demonstrated or conceived can only be so by an actual representation of sense or memory and everything depends upon the exactitude and fidelity of this representation, which will, doubtless, acquire more promptitude and facility through frequent repetition, but which habit cannot transform into a pure mechanism.

The very names associated with the figures and different modifications of space, serve to give a useful hold, a necessary support to representative memory.   Here the sign and the idea are so well made for each other that once united they cannot be separated; their mutual correspondence is always prompt, exact, infallible.   The simplicity and the symmetry of the figures strikes the sight as distinctly as sound strikes the ear; those perceptions which are equally clear, will become equally persistant.   Likewise very young children are seen to learn very easily to remember and apply the names of the simple figures of geometry.   Afterwards if they recall the name, we ascertain immediately whether they have the idea by making them draw its object, an inestimable advantage and one peculiar to this system of ideas.   Happy the children who have the foundation of their memory furnished with words, the representations of which they can also imagine or delineate! In minds which an early habit may have inclined in this way, the signs would of themselves immediately tend to be combined with ideas, as ideas with signs, and vague or empty terms would not find room to lodge there and would be rejected as foreign matter.

II. In surveying the principal classes of our ideas, we have found those which are the most adapted to give rise to and develop habits of representative memory, to become, so to say, the nutritive milk of intelligence.   This object is so important that I ask permission to dwell upon it some moments longer. Moreover, I do not think that I am deviating from the question or the purpose of the philosophers who have proposed it; and to what in the final result ought the knowledge of our habits to lead us, if not to the means of forming good ones?

Since intelligence is entirely in the faculty of representation, it is to the development of this faculty that the primary education ought to be entirely directed; it is a question of forming a habit which is an indispensible *condition* of its exercise.

In rejecting with the greatest care all signs or formulas and exercises of mechanical recitation (as well as everything that could give to sensibility a precocious and dangerous stimulation, carry, in some way, in the organ of thought a vicious principle of excitation, and accustom it to the vague, the mysterious, to phantoms of every kind, etc.), the primary education would be naturally circumscribed within the circumference of simple, clear, determinate ideas, or at least of those always susceptible of the most exact determination. The study of arithmetic, of elementary geometry, added to the constant practice of drawing (which ought to be the first written language), would furnish a fundamental basis of the whole edifice of subsequent knowledge. But there would still be precautions to take in order to establish this basis. It is not enough to be informed about the quality of the materials. It is further necessary to know how to adjust them suitably to each other.

I would require, for example, (and for the reasons previously announced) that the first notions of geometry should precede the knowledge and the practice of our signs or of ordinary methods of calculation; the ideas even of numbers might be representative (for example, taking one line for unity, dividing it in equal parts, adding it to itself, etc.). Numeration understood, children should not be detained long upon the operations with signs for fear that they should degenerate into a blind routine. The theory of relations should be demonstrated on the figures themselves, according to Euclid's method, which could be much abridged and simplified. In a word, everything that could be demonstrated in perceptions or ideas, should always be done in this way. We would pass from the representation of sense to the sign of memory, from the concrete to the abstract, only with deliberation and circumspection, and the sign, having become abstract, should still be frequently translated into and brought back to the sensible, which was its origin.

It should be only after having thus put to continual proofs the representative faculty, after being well assured of its exercise, that one could apply it without danger and successfully to the quick and easy procedure of our methods of calculation. Thus the advances of the individual would follow almost the same order as those of the learned; the youthful intelligence would daily extend its powers through exercising them and when it would come to the use of levers, we would recognize, according to the way in which it would avail itself of them, its proper and native vigor.

In geometric demonstrations (the length and difficulties of which are graded according to the extent of the thinking ability), I would require the pupil, instead of always having the figure before his eyes, to contract the habit of perceiving its proportions in the picture preserved and retraced by his memory.   It would be easy to judge (from the way in which he would express himself in demonstrating) of the degree of precision and exactitude of his ideas.   It is thus, and not with words alone, that real memory is cultivated.

The same object would be fulfilled through the practice of drawing, if the pupil is instructed in *mentally* retracing and copying the models which have made an impression on him in nature.   He would thus form a habit of looking more attentively to remember and imitate better.   Thus perception and memory would uphold and sustain each other.

Finally, whatever be the system of ideas with which we would be concerned in the process of time, the pupil *of reason* would always be obliged to retain and render a precise and faithful account of the ideas themselves, of their connection, of their order of concatenation, without ever being reduced to the expressions used by the teachers or the authors, rejecting purely mechanical recitations as carefully as a pedantic method ordinarily sets about to multiply them.

I ask pardon for this digression, if it is one, in behalf of the motive which suggested it. But, before returning to the precise limits of my subject, I beg to be permitted to make some further reflections upon the relations which the use of a particular language would have with the habits of representative memory.

III. The practice of languages which unite the double likeness of signs with each other and with ideas, seconds in the most fortunate way the formation and the development of the habits of which we are speaking. When the word depicts the idea and the idea depicts the fact, these three elements, united in one and the same bundle afford each other a reciprocal support in thought. If similar ideas are represented by sensible forms or word-endings of articulate terms, if the identical combinations of facts are depicted in those of the same characters or elementary sounds, memory will follow the easy declivity of the habits of the ear and the voice. There is no mechanism to fear here; when the end is certain and the road is sure, what does one risk in allowing oneself to be drawn to it?

The language of modern chemistry is well fitted to serve as an example of this point. We remember its terms with as much facility as we apprehend the ideas; the former are never isolated from the latter, and we can no more learn the language without the science than the science without the language. Thus, the more familiar we are with the latter and the more disgust we feel for the vague, delusive, meaningless expressions of the old method of teaching, the more we form a habit, a need for the exact determination of the signs that we make use of and of the ideas that they express.

Also the study of pneumatic chemistry[1] seems to me to concur happily with the means previously indicated to form habits of representative memory.

Although our usual languages, designed to represent and express all sorts of ideas and combinations as extensive as they

[1] Presumably this is what is usually called pneumatics.—Tr.

are heterogeneous, do not permit this exact analogy which belongs only to sciences the object of which is circumscribed within one and the same kind of elements or within a uniform order of combinations and relations; nevertheless, in comparing these deverse languages, it is readily seen that they combine different characteristics, more or less apt to favor or to disturb the tranquillity and precision of representation of ideas.

Discretion in the order, sobriety in the figures, precision and clearness in the expression, uniformity in the order of construction; articulations not too rough, not too soft, nor too flattering to the ear—such characteristics will be able to reinforce the representative faculty with all that they take away from the vivacity of the imagination and energy of feeling.

Fixedness of construction ought to have an especially marked influence on the habits of memory of which we are speaking. This faculty, in fact, finds double exercise in the operation which consists in recalling at the same time both the words and the order in which they should be arranged; the habit of this fixed order should even be so much the more difficult to form in proportion as it tends to put a restraint upon the imagination and to moderate its flights. But, as soon as it is contracted, thought complies with the rule, follows it without constraint and with a sort of necessity. Doubtless, the advantages which result from this voluntary subjection are indeed preferable to a disorderly and dissolute freedom.

The principal image, being at first represented by its sign (which is brought forward first in the *direct* order of construction), thought is fixed upon this image and stops to contemplate it, as the eye is fixed upon the most striking external object before taking a survey of the details which surround it. Intellectual details are likewise depicted in the portraiture of speech according to their importance, are reflected by the light, are examined in detail and in order, without hurry or impatience to reach a desired, unknown, or more attractive term, inducing it to skip over the intermediary terms which separate it from its goal.

Exalted sensibility and rebellious imagination sometimes tend to upset the rational order and to influence speech. A stronger habit restrains them; it raises a momentary conflict and from the opposition of forces results equilibrium and calm. We speak indeed only in so far as we have self-command. We learn to master ourselves in learning to speak well, and speech itself reveals disorder and emptiness of thought. Happy the people with whom the habits of language may thus be identified with those of order, wisdom, and reason!

The repeated activity of representative memory should have upon the fixed tendencies of thought the same effects which in general a moderate and justly proportional use of their powers—which leaves no part of them inactive and which never exceeds them—has upon the sensory and motor organs. As the characteristic function of intelligence is to circumscribe images nicely and to attach them to signs, it will always fulfil this function in a manner so much the more imperturbable in proportion as it has acquired early a habit, a necessity (but it is to this important end that all the means indicated in this chapter tend); the continuity of such an activity puts to good advantage the parts of the central organ, multiplies and fortifies their connections, does not let any of them predominate, but, on the contrary, maintains them in that equilibrium, that exact correspondance, which constitutes true intellectual capacity, and forms, so to say, the even temper of thought.

CHAPTER V

How the Habits of Language or the Frequent Repetition of the Same Terms are First the Foundation of Our Judgments of "Real Existence" and Then the Cause of Transforming Those Which We May Make upon the Relations of Our Terms or Ideas

All contemporaneous impressions, all movements which are continually repeated together, are so closely joined and contract such an adherence that they can no longer be isolated, but incessantly summon each other, replace each other, and often are confused in thought. The same law of association, the same power of habit which first creates natural signs for us (see Chapters II and III, first section) and then conceals from us their functions, directs and modifies in the same way the use of artificial signs of language.

I. These last signs are only movements or characters instituted by us and superadded to our impressions, to distinguish them better and particularly to adapt them to *recall* (see the first chapter of this section). But when an old and long-standing habit cemented the bond and incrusted, so to say, the label in the object which it was merely designed to mark, the articulation or the recall of the word, the perception of the object or the appearance of the image, evoke each other so infallibly and with such a rapidity, they are so thoroughly involved in the same simultaneous act of motor activity, that they appear to be identified in the same subject and to participate in the same *essence*.

This is why the conventional signs seem most often to have with the objects or the ideas that they express this same relation of *inherence* which makes us judge color to be in space and tactile modifications to be in the resisting object.

This is why this syllable *iron*, for example, seems to the man in the street as inherent in the metal as the solidity, the dull color, and other properties, the sum total of which this word expresses; and finally why, as Locke has observed, the one who says, "This is iron," thinks that he expresses something more than a name and that he designates perhaps the intimate nature of this substance.

If this illusory judgment, which is founded entirely on an old habit, can thus identify arbitrary signs with the nature of the objects or impressions themselves, which have a basis in resistance, how should it fail to have a tendency to merge wholly abstract ideas and archetypes with the terms which in reality serve them as a sole support in memory? This is why, on the one hand, signs lend to ideas a sort of material reality and why, on the other hand, ideas considered as real entities in their turn communicate a magic power to those conventional terms, from which they are inseparable. This is why the individual may recall words and believe that he receives ideas, as by inspiration, why he can operate on empty signs and believe that they express eternal verities; this is why one succeeds in forgetting and misconstruing the common origin of signs and ideas; why, blended together and disguised by each other, the phantom and its term seem equally inspired in our souls or seem to come down completely formed from the heart of the Divinity.

This illusion or this prejudice, which leads us to attribute external reality to all that is invested with a sign in our memory, is at once connected with a profound habit of our judgments, with the first associations of our language, and with those usual forms which we never cease using and whose motives are hidden from us by the very familiarity we have with them.

Our primary signs (useful and real) were at first only simple appellations attached to sensory or directly representable objects. Afterwards when the improvements of our faculties extended the functions of these signs until they expressed what is called mental insight, until they determine the consequences of operations and abstract or complex notions of every kind, etc., the first crease was formed, the imagination had contracted the habit of vibrating in some way under the pulsating force of articulated sounds. It will thus still tend to convert them to its own use. For a long time, however, and perhaps always, this lively faculty will proceed to falsify the pure conceptions of the understanding and will respond by some more or less vague representation, to written or spoken terms which make them sensible to sight or hearing. This is why the signs of the most archetypal ideas, the names of spiritual substances and of invisible powers, are always connected in the minds of children and ignorant people (and sometimes even of the learned) with some sensory model, some more or less material image; this again is why we involuntarily attach a physical appearance to the unknown person or object, the names of which we hear pronounced.

But, by virtue of the first habit itself (or, if you will, of our natural way of perceiving), no object can be represented with any clearness or any force to the imagination, without being put or imagined actually in relief outside of the Ego, who contemplates it in some part of space or time more or less distant, early, contracted, etc. Hence, a prime cause sufficient to found the judgment of real existence, which will afterwards gain credit by repetition, as we shall soon see.

Let one detach, for example, from various individual objects compared with one another, a certain number of properties or sensory qualities, in order to form from them the common type of a species, a genus, etc., the new artificial compound has no longer any real original, any *substratum* in nature. It has support only in the sign which gives a purchase to thought and often a motive power to imagination. As soon as this faculty takes possession of the abstract term, it transforms it again, brings it back to the sensory, creates for it another *substratum*, which it places outside of the visible world, in those regions of *essences*, *substantial forms*, etc., where phantoms take the place of reality. Habits of language, in agreement with the imagination which has originated them, afterwards give great consistency to all the illusory judgments which it has instigated.

Our abstract terms enter the forms of our languages in the same way as physical substantives. As subjects of propositions, the verb affirms of them in the same attributes, the same absolute properties, as of real objects; moreover, our expressions, which are almost always figurative, give them a body to animate them, represent them to us active, moving and feeling like ourselves. How could this likeness, enduring in the forms, fail to delude the judgment? How, in short, could the habits of thought fail to be moulded upon those of speech?

How many times does it not happen that the determinative formula of existence (at first applied to that which is, as well as to that which is not; to what we perceive, as well as to what we imagine; to real products of nature, as well as to the most arbitrary creations of our fancy) ends by drawing our judgments into the blind mechanism of words and bases faith upon the old and frequent repetition of the vainest formulas? . . . . Here is the too fertile source of a multitude of prejudices; here habit gives to the signs of memory a power of the same nature as, but indeed superior to, the one which it gave to the signs of imagination (see Chapter III, first section).

II. Aside from the signs of language, habits of judgment and imagination should conform most frequently to those which nature follows in the production of phenomena. It is, doubtless, necessary that facts accompany or follow each other many times and in a sufficiently constant order, in order that their images form this close and fixed association with each other which determines practical *faith*, takes the place of all reasoning, of all comparison of chances, of all calculation of probabilities.

The intervention of speech impresses quite another characteristic on those associations; first it accelerates them through the effect which it produces on thought (see Chapter I, second section). Then it cements them by supplementing the rarity of phenomena through its free activity, by forcing in some way the frequent appearance of their images through voluntary repetition. Finally, it gives support to the enunciation of the judgment and the copula, which unites two contingent facts, imparts to them by repetition the characteristic of fixed existence, of necessary connection. Then the real world disappears before the imaginary world; the individual indeed believes more in what he says, hears and incessantly repeats than in what he sees and touches. Everything is under the sway of the word! . . . .

Let us here distinguish the cases where the force of adhesion and the stubbornness of the judgment are founded at the same time upon habits of speech and upon those of the imagination (which receive from it more vividness and persistency)[1] from those in which habits of speech alone are dominant, where mechanical belief rests solely on the frequent and constant repetition of the same terms devoid of sense.

Let a liar, for example, end by being the dupe of his own stories; let a head of a sect, after having for a long time professed error with perfect knowledge of what he was doing, become finally illuminated in good earnest by the best faith in the world; or again let popular rumors, new improbabilities, unfounded reputations, etc., pass without examination as so many acknowledged points, *articles of faith*, which it is no longer permitted to question, captivate everyone by a magic power and persist only because a thousand mouths repeat them, because the ear is accustomed to hear them and the imagination to adopt them. . . . . We recognize in most of these examples the foundation and the power of a double habit. But what sort of roots can these formulas in the imagination, these words fantastically associated together have, which, repeated from infancy and transformed into habits of mechanical or sensory memory, become the object of a kind of purely verbal faith, in support of which men have been seen to be carried to all extremes and to sacrifice even their lives? Upon what shall

[1] See Chapter IV, first section, and Chapter III, second section.

we ground this power of certain meaningless words which sectarians incessantly have on the tip of their tongue to corroborate their faith, which they proclaim with emphasis and hurl confidently at the heads of their enemies, as if sure of overwhelming them?

To conceive the extraordinary effects which are connected principally with habits of language, let us first recall what has previously been observed (Chapter III and at the beginning of this one) of the origin and transformation of most of our abstract or archetypal terms. It is when their conventional character as *signs* is most forgotten and ignored that they frequently acquire a power which is marvelous, like those ambitious and powerful persons who assume under a vague title a limitless authority which they would not obtain under a definite and familiar name.

Let us again recall (and this will apply to the most ordinary cases and to the influence of habit exclusively) what was said (Chapter II) of the mechanism of memory.

What is a judgment enunciated in empty terms or ones to which no meaning is attached, but an activity of mechanical memory, which traces again those terms with the assurance of an old habit, in the same order in which they are always followed, in this fixed, necessary order, the determination of which the ear and the voice have contracted so well, in which one can no longer change nor substitute one word for another? Try to put, for example, the sign of *negation* in place of *affirmation*, without tormenting the ear as if by a dissonance or without producing that disagreeable surprise which is experienced when an habitual movement, which had already received its impetus, is suddenly stopped.

Since, in the case of which we are speaking, the terms are devoid of any idea for the one who uses them, it matters little whether they are susceptible of a real meaning, of any representative value whatsoever, in ordinary or philosophical usage, or whether they are absolutely destitute of it by their nature; the form of the judgment will be equally mechanical in the two cases. (It is thus that we shall from this time forward characterize the kind of judgment in question.)

Let a child, for example, recite his catechism or the table of Pythagoras, without any rudiment of numeration; he will believe or say that $9 \times 9 = 81$ (as he has been taught to say), that three make only one; he would judge likewise that nine times nine make any other number whatsoever, if he had repeated this latter affirmation the same number of times.

Let us observe, however, that *mechanical* judgment must be distinguished from simple recall or from the physical articulation of words. This last act, having become, so to say, automatic through the effect of habit, seems foreign to the functions characteristic of intelligence. But judgment always presupposes a sort of acquiescence accorded to the *statement*. Thought adopts it, rests upon it, excludes its opposite. But this acquiescence is not only founded on the present and momentary act of recall, but, further, on the remembrance of having constantly repeated and always in the same way in all circumstances, the same terms, the expression of the same relation.

This being granted, we see how each repetition, added to those which precede, influences the judgment with this sum of forces, which increases in proportion as we advance. When we are far from the origin, we do not remember, do not ask whether we ever had a motive for judging or thinking in this way; but we know only that we have always believed and we continue without power or wish to investigate. . . . . Thus the accumulated reports of our memories determine conviction in the same way that various witnesses who agree establish a fact, although they often base their testimony on one another's word. In both cases, votes, which should be *weighed*, are *counted*. . . . . Thus is born and strengthened habitual belief, blind faith! obstinate faith! which, to the shame of the human spirit, exerts a much more general influence than the authority of reason and all the splendor of evidence!

It is clear indeed that a single mechanical judgment, once adopted, must soon summon and attract a multitude of others;

that thus, the tendency to judge without examination, to give credit to words and to place reliance on them, being incessantly fortified by the facility and ease of its exercise, must finally become invincible. Since it is the memory of words which furnishes blind credulity with proper food, we are now still better able to see how sinister this exclusive culture of which we were speaking (Chapter II) must be to reason.

III. When the association of signs and ideas has been regularly made according to the conditions set forth (Chapters I and IV of this section); when the use of any abstract or complex term whatsoever has been preceded by deliberate operations which are able to determine its status, and fix its value; it is never in vain that these signs and sounds strike the eye and the ear. They re-echo in the depths of the organ of thought cause images or elementary terms to spring from it, which are confided to the agency of representative memory, which, in turn restoring them with fidelity and so to speak in the same terms, determines new evaluations or comparisons and gives real and solid motives to those judgments which I shall call *reflective.*

But must these comparisons and judgments always be founded upon the same operations? Can this precious evidence, which throws light on their origin, always accompany them in their repetitions? Will it then be necessary to return incessantly to verify elements already known and appreciated? But how can one walk or run in this vast field open to our perfectibility, if it is necessary ever to look back and retrace one's steps?

What will then supplement those regular operations, those first grounds of judgment, when habit will have made them disappear? What can take the place of the past intuition of truth when other pressing needs will have driven one from the source and will not permit one to return there?

In the repetition of *mechanical judgment*, the remembrance of having always believed without any proof takes the place of evidence. In the repetition of *reflective judgment*, the remembrance of having once perceived this evidence replaces the immediate perception of it; and the individual who judges from the label still believes without examination, because he recalls having already examined, estimated, known, and because this primitive authority suffices to convince him. Here then, as in the other case, belief is founded upon the report of a series of *witnesses*. But the first affirms what he has seen and he is worthy of trust; moreover, its source alone has changed and confidence always increases by reason of the number of the witnesses. Perhaps there is no philosopher who does not believe more firmly the ancient truth, which he has often repeated (although without actual demonstration) than in the very instant of proof: there thus always enters a little mechanism in judgments and habit cannot quite lose its rights.

But our reflective judgments are not only confirmed by being repeated. It is clear, moreover, through what has just been said, that they change in nature in changing motives. If perception of evidence constitutes reflective judgment, habit, which substitutes memories for perception, will transform it into judgment of reminiscence.

This transformation seems to me to be referred to two modes of the influence of habit which we have already recognized in other classes of phenomena.

1. Uncontested posssession brings indifference in its train; whatever be the end to which we may tend, activity is entirely in pursuit. It languishes and is extinguished in enjoyment. This is true in the intellectual and non-physical world as in the sensuous and physical.

The acquisition of this truth, which excited such lively raptures, cost so much care and work, is soon going to attract only the most superficial attention. It was an *end* and will become a *means*, an *instrument*. It was on the altar and will no longer serve except for a step; the terms which express it, instead of exciting that energetic activity which came from their strangeness, will be glanced over by thought, as familiar objects on which the distracted eye no longer deigns to rest;

they will with difficulty determine this slight judgment of reminiscence (see the end of Chapter III of the first section)
which hurries the journey instead of delaying it.

2. The confidence which we accord to what we have often
repeated as to what is always reproduced before our eyes in the
same way, makes us consider every new examination absolutely
useless and place our practical consent on a basis quite foreign
to reflection. Here habit again modifies the judgments which
do not emerge from the confines of our ideas, as those which
bear on the facts of the outside world.

We await with perfect security phenomena which constantly
succeed each other; qualities found at various times in an
object are supposed to dwell there always. We employ the
instrument which has served us to produce certain effects,
with the certitude of always drawing the same advantage from
it, etc. What is the need of calculating contrary chances, of
making new experiments, of again examining before acting?

Likewise, have not these terms in which we have recognized
such and such elements, such and such relations, by a preliminary analysis, well or badly made, invariably kept the same
value as the same external forms? Why lose time in useless
verifications which can tell us only what we already know? It
is indeed simpler to trust to the testimony of our memories.

We shall discuss in the following chapter the results of this
hurry, of this habitual confidence. Let us here distinguish the
cases where it may be justified from those in which it offers
various kinds of dangers.

When terms are susceptible of exact and easy determination,
when the homogeneity of their elements has permitted a more
or less perfect analogy to be established between them, when
the series, the operations in which they enter, carry in themselves
their means of verification, when, in short, it is only a question
of determining the relations of our signs with each other and
with our ideas, without any application to that which exists
outside of us, the immutability of these relations, the real
and constant value of these terms, regularly established, enable

us to dispense with going into the details of their first formation and give most frequently to simple remembrance an authority as legitimate as to direct perception.

It is then that our first judgments take a character of fixedness, of absolute necessity, which determines their extension to a multitude of particular cases, without its being necessary to scrutinize incessantly their original foundation. Then the operations which assign them as motives are often carried out without danger by a rapid mechanism, as sure as instinct, and habits seconded by a precious similarity can themselves become means and instruments of science.

But in most cases and in almost all classes of ideas, aside from that of simple modes (see Chapter IV) the diversity, the complexity of the elements which are subsumed under individual terms, the vagueness and indetermination of which the nature of their object renders them susceptible, always commands distrust, exacts an attention so much the more sustained and evaluations so much the more frequent in proportion as there are more chances for hidden error in the first instituting of the signs and more danger of uncertainty in their successively repeated use. But habit, which excludes this attention in order often to substitute for it a blind mechanism, can lead us astray in various ways.

If we first took a vague report, a false glimmering, for evidence itself, memory which henceforth takes the place of every other proof, reproducing the same illusion, will give it more consistency and will deprive us immediately of every means of recognizing it and dissipating it. Has the first reflective judgment been founded upon real evidence? The terms which express it may have changed value. Repeating themselves they have perhaps lost some of their old elements or gained new ones. Then, on the one hand, habit makes the immutability of the relations perceived in the first place to be presupposed. On the other hand, a contradictory judgment is established about different relations expressed nevertheless by

the same terms.   The *pro* and the *con*, opposed to each other
with equal force, are neutralised and scepticism triumphs.

The too prompt conversion of our reflective judgments into
remembrances is thus indeed more often harmful than advan-
tageous to our progress (as we shall still better see in the following chapter).   Why do we fear to bring back our grounds of
belief frequently for a new examination?   We shall consolidate
them, if they are well founded.   We shall strengthen them,
if they rest falsely.   We shall save in any case the independence
of our judgments by snatching them from a too rapid descent,
which ever tends to drag them along; and obstinate habit will
not force us to judge wrongly all our life because we judged
wrongly once.

CHAPTER VI

Continuation of the Preceding

CONCERNING THE REPETITION OF THE SAME SERIES OF JUDGMENTS; THE INFLUENCE OF HABIT UPON THE OPERATIONS AND METHODS OF REASONING; CONCLUSION OF THE WORK

I. We can only reason, as we compute, with the help of conventional signs; this truth has been too clearly expounded by Condillac and the philosophers who followed him to need new proofs. The whole operation of reasoning consists in recalling the signs in their order and with the precise value which has previously been assigned to them; to *operate* is to *act*; to act is to *move*; but the individual moves when he *recalls*, and he recalls only in moving.

Judgment is not the operation itself, it differs from it as the conduct of the organ differs from perception, as effort from its result; but the individual mistaking his own action, which has become extremely rapid and easy, incessantly confounds it with its result: such is the law of habit; the language of metaphysicians is itself a speaking proof of it.

What is true of a single judgment is true also of any series of judgments bound together. Never is there anything but the active faculty of recall, or memory, which is truly active. It alone directs all our reasonings, following its habits; which justifies the importance which we have attached to a thorough knowledge of these different habits, since on that depends all that remains to be said.

In the recall of ordered series of terms or ideas, we have scarcely considered up to this point the effects of repetition except in the modes of succession, the degrees of facility and promptitude, the precise or confused limitation of those terms, taken individually in the chain of which they form a part. Let us now apply these first results to the comparison of the same terms, to their similitudes, to the perception of their relations, to the summation of the series which they form.

1. In the execution of every voluntary movement, there is a moderate degree of effort, which renders action precise and easy without hiding it from consciousness, and a higher degree, which, hiding from the individual the part that he plays in it, tends to make it automatic. The same holds good of the recall of series of signs. A certain quick succession, a certain effort facilitate comparisons and the perception of relations and give thought the necessary activity; but beyond a certain limit, all is obscured and merged, the operations as well as the judgments or the series of judgments which result from them.

When we perform an operation or when we wish to follow a bit of reasoning for the first time, our uncertain memory is at first exercised only slowly and with difficulty; preoccupied at the same time with the recall of the signs, of the order to observe between them, and of their intrinsic value, it is troubled and goes astray in this simple task. Since motor activity exerts itself too much on each term, there does not remain sufficient energy to apprehend them altogether and include them in one common activity; or indeed, these terms being separated by too great intervals, one is already far from thought when the other occupies and engrosses it. In these two cases there may indeed be terms separately distinct, but no perceived relations, no series of connected judgments, no deductions.

By repeating various times the same operation, the activity of memory is strengthened and accelerated; the simple recall of signs is no longer a labor; they are brought together and appear, one might say, under similar aspects, and gaps between them are filled. They are already from this point of view in exactly that degree of proximity, which enables them to be compared and to be framed in the same picture. Soon they will pervade and interpenetrate one another; they will no longer be a series or a collection of distinct terms, but a single whole, a concrete mass, of which the elements, closely joined, will afterwards perhaps be proof against our means of analysis.

That is why, in the most complex and at first the most laborious reasoning, after frequent repetition, the beginning and the end seem to touch and to connect directly with each other, so unsteady has the intermediate chain become, so great are the readiness and facility with which it is performed! Thus, the genius, strong in his habits—happily persistant— goes with the rapidity of the eagle over the longest series of propositions, brings together masses of ideas, piles them high and, a new giant, scales the heavens. . . . . We shall not, however, exaggerate this power of the genius too much; undoubtedly he includes a multitude of objects in a single glance, but he perhaps assumes even more of them than he sees; he counts on the numerous reports of his memory; these are so many witnesses whose fidelity he has at various times ascertained and who enable him to dispense with new examinations. In adding what precedes to what has been said on the same subject in the last chapter, we see how habit modifies and transforms the series of reflective judgments, now in accelerating and facilitating the operations which precede and motivate them to the point of rendering them insensible and of confusing many of them in one, now in altogether annulling these operations and in letting the result only subsist as a simple remembrance. These two effects, which incessantly coöperate to increase the readiness and nimbleness of reasoning, further explain to us why we are so often blind to its nature and its forms, to its reality and the necessity of the operations which order it.

2. When a chain of reasoning has become very familiar to us by frequent repetition, we neglect the operations which motivated it in the beginning and by dint of neglecting them or of going over them quickly, we end by forgetting them, misunderstanding them, and considering them absolutely useless. This is what warrants so many ellipses in the forms of reasoning as in those of usual and familiar discourse.

Indeed, what is the use of descanting on a long series of terms when one is accustomed to understand from the first word? Can the impatience to arrive at an expected conclusion forseen in advance and toward which one can leap in a single bound, admit of all these digressions, all this display of intermediaries? They will be suppressed at first by design, afterwards involuntarily, and the premises are going to dissolve in the conclusion, as various words are subsumed in a single one by long usage. But is there not danger that these omissions, consecrated by habit, will introduce into the foundations of logic the same abuses, the same obscurities, the same forgetfulness of first principles, that they have often occasioned in the forms and roots of our languages?

How shall we afterwards attain what is far beyond the reach of our immediate perception, after having destroyed the path which could surely have led us there? How shall we determine very precise measurements, when we have lost the common standard? How shall we expose sophism and paradox, which are hid by being repressed? How shall we show the emptiness of grave maxims, which seem to say much in a few words and which it is most often only necessary to develop, to translate into exact forms in order to recognize their vagueness and insignificance?

3. If there were not complex terms, there would not be useful reasoning and real deduction.

The whole difficulty of these operations always consists in coming back from the compound expression to its elements, as from an equation to its roots, from any function whatsoever to its derivatives (or reciprocally, etc.). This difficulty would disappear if we knew how to or if we could, in all cases, observe and likewise note down what has happened in the regular combination of first elements.

But preconceptions first hinder us from making all these observations and habit afterwards brings forward an invincible obstacle, through the ready mechanism that it introduces into the operations (see the first article).

What would happen if we received these complex terms all formed, if they became extremely familiar to us by long repetition, if we always considered them and used them *en masse*, so to say, without dreaming of going into the details of their composition, perhaps even without suspecting it? How then should this term, which is articulated in an instant, fail to seem simple to thought, since it is *one* for the voice and the hearing? How could it ever become the subject of an analysis? And it is this, in fact, which renders the use of this method so laborious and so distasteful to most men. To go back to it, they must begin by distrusting their habits, and how uncommon such distrust is!

Even when the complex term has been regularly formed, thought is doubtless attached to a certain fixed order of combinations, memory is afterwards subjected to it through frequent repetitions and has contracted the habit of always retracing in the same order the combined elements. By virtue of this habit, there will henceforth be only this one method of composition or analysis which seems practical. Among all the other possible combinations of elements, two by two, three by three, etc., we can no longer see any except that which we are accustomed to follow. Thus, with a sufficiently complete knowledge of the elements which compose an idea or a term, we can be really very far from appreciating all its fecundity, in the same way that the owner of a large and fertil field does not know its riches, when a blind routine in the manner of cultivating it hinders him from turning it to account.

How many times may it not happen that with all the data for solving a question we fall short of the goal, because the true road which could lead there is different from the one which habit indicates as the only good one and to which a sort of blind routine obstinately draws us?

For example, he who has always considered the number 9 as resulting from the combination of 5 and 4, might be ignorant that it could likewise be reached by that of 6 and 3, and reject these last numbers as not being suitable to form what he wishes

to obtain, etc.   It is thus dangerous to be enslaved, in the composition of terms or ideas, by too uniform an order; for, once
it should be transformed into habit and mechanism, it would
become absolutely exclusive, it would hold us enclosed in the
narrow sphere of the same operations and thus limit all further
progress.   We are so inclined to measure possibilities on the
scale of our habits and to believe that there is nothing outside
of our familiar system!

We perceive still better here how fatal to our progress this
prompt conversion of our reflective judgments into simple
remembrance may be, this absolute confidence in our memories,
this indifference in regard to old principles which we consider
certain and perfectly known, because they have been frequently
repeated.   What we can know, as Condillac has said, is enclosed in what we already do know: that then is what it is
necessary to seek.   But, after all that we have just remarked
about the effects of habit, it is clear that it is that which puts
the greatest obstacles to this search.   Indifference in regard to
acquired ideas, nimbleness, extreme readiness in surveying
them and passing over them, blindness as to their complexity
or the varities of the combinations of which their elements are
susceptible, absolute bondage to the same routines. . . . .
Can we imbibe new knowledge from what we have, can we lay
hold of supports there to raise us higher?

4. If the mechanism, into which all our repeated operations
incessantly degenerate, did not obscure their origin, nature
and number; if the familiarity of the terms was not illusorily
confounded with exact, infallible knowledge; if independence of
judgment could be reconciled with the facility and readiness
which pulls it along, doubtless the influence of habit upon all
our progress would be certain, pure, and unmixed.   But why is
it necessary that what is gained in speed and in extent, is so
often lost in force and depth?   Why, after having attached
wings to thought, does not habit permit it to direct its own
flight, instead of holding it obstinately fixed in the same
direction?

Such is, in fact, the most fatal result of a long and too exclusive repetition of the same operations, of the same procedure whatsoever it may be; thought can no longer change its habitual gait and resists everything that might distract it, as the pendulum does not deviate from the predetermined arc to which gravity keeps it.

It is by such a chain that habit holds back such a large number of individuals servilly attached to practices, maxims, methods, of which they have made routines; it is this which, joining the force of inertia to the activity of interest and self-esteem, excited so many prejudices against the most useful discoveries, so often delayed their happy effects, gave rise to so many hates and persecutions of those geniuses, the honor of their species, who forcing down the barriers of old antipathies, knew how to establish new principles upon new facts or unravel from old principles and facts, which were believed to be well known, a host of different aspects which extend their fruitfulness. It is habit which after having founded abstract principles upon the mechanical repetition of the same formulas, puts them afterwards beyond all discussion, and incessantly cries out that it is necessary to beware of submitting them to a new examination, and thus perpetuates all the erroneous consequences of false principles, or presses back within narrow limits the applications of those which may be true and useful in themselves.

It is habit which, accrediting through long usage so many pernicious methods of classification, so often causes nature to be measured on an imaginary scale and, after false observations have fixed error in the nomenclature or the language of a science, it is still habit which perpetuates the error by the repetition of the language.

In short it is habit, which, taking possession of the products of the imagination, of those truly *archetypal* ideas, to which systematic minds force future facts to conform, often gives to vain hypotheses a consistency, a predominance which all the evidence of reality, the most authentic proofs of the senses and of reason, cannot counterbalance.

5. As habit makes thought inert before all which might lead it from its guidance, so it gives it activity to apprehend and appropriate all that conforms to it. The foundation of ideas which are formed and inlaid, so to say, in the central organ, may be said to attract by a sort of affinity all that maintains with it some relations of analogy, as it exerts a repelling force upon what is dissimilar to it.

Let us recall here what we have already observed (Chapter II of this section). The transition from a series of ideas, of terms or, in general, of movements to a new and different series can only be facilitated through the analogy or partial identity which prevails between elementary terms of the two series. The individual then, operating or moving partly as he has just operated, does not have to use altogether new endeavors and finds rest in uniformity.

Memory will retain and thus learn to retrace the elements of a given complex idea with so much the more ease in proportion as this idea is the more analogous or in proportion as a greater number of elements which it contains is identical with the most familiar system of ideas. For the same reason the relations of the new idea will be determined with more promptitude and precision; for the more terms that occur in its analysis identical with those which are already known and previously verified, the more judgments of memory there are which, being inserted between reflective judgments, rest the attention and hurry along with the rapidity of acquired habits, toward the last result or the final conclusion.

This is what happens, especially in operations which we execute upon the complex ideas of simple modes: as in this case all the elements are similar, we are easily led from one combination to another by the great chain of identity. If we wish to analyse or compare with each other ideas of a higher order, we do not fail to come soon to terms already evaluated at which we stop or of which we make use (as known) in the course of the operation, which can thus acquire an unlimited speed.

It is thus by analogy and by it alone that the sphere of our habits is extended and successively embraces different systems of ideas. It is analogy which makes the transition from the known to the unknown so gentle, from that which is familiar to that which is new, over which thought, so to say, glides unconsciously. We learn and we think that all we do is to remember. We are in a new world, and it seems that we have not left the precincts of our habits. This is why good teachers, imitating wise nature, lead us by degrees from dark to light and insensibly accustom our weak eyes to look at the truth. This is why Socrates, acting as a midwife to minds, believed in the pre-existence of this intellectual germ, which the efficacy of his skill caused to be born.

But, independently of this analogy or partial identity which unites through common habits different systems of ideas and prepares an easy transition from the one to the other, should there not be still another kind of analogy or resemblance in the order and arrangement of these ideas or their terms, which being reproduced in a uniform manner in the expression of all our judgments or reasonings whatsoever, would give us a general habit of the art of reasoning, like that of calculating? Are there not methods, instruments, the use of which we can acquire by repeated exercise and which serve us afterwards as levers adapted to raise, so to say, every kind of mass, to bring it again to our understanding and to suit every kind of material to it? Of what do these methods consist? What are the cases in which they can guide us in the right way or lead us in false directions, give rise to and strengthen good intellectual habits or produce and nourish bad ones? Such are the important subjects which I should have liked to examine in some detail and which my powers do not permit me to do more than skim over in this last article.

II. In all reasoning, in every regular deduction, the memory fulfills two essential but very distinct functions, as we have already observed; to wit, to recall or to represent with each sign the bundle of ideas, or at least the principal ideas which it expresses; in the second place, to recall the series of signs in a predetermined order.

One of these functions can be exercised without the other, as in fact occurs very often: the signs may be recalled in their order very regularly without being connected to any idea; in this case, memory and judgment are mechanical. On the other hand, memory is representative and judgments are reflective, when the terms are recalled with their value, although they may not be regularly linked with one another.

The order or the arrangement of the terms constitutes the form of the reasoning; the representation of the ideas, allied to the signs, is their essence or the subject matter.

Since we can adapt different words to the same tune, various pictures to the same frame, a host of empty or significant words to the same grammatical order, the subject matter of the reasoning may vary in an infinity of ways, while always keeping a form agreed upon.

Now, what always remains the same in the midst of the variations, cannot fail to be considered substantial; and that explains the excessive importance attached to the form of reasoning, which almost always ends by having the advantage over the subject matter. In the same manner as the rhythm, which is continually reproduced in each verse, is remembered before the words, the forms of reasoning may also become a habit of memory first and be fixed there, so to say, as a corner-stone to which the subject matter will afterwards be joined, when it can.

But all the terms which are in memory apart from ideas, belong to the mechanism of this faculty. We can thus say that the form of reasoning, and all the habitual operations, of which it is the exclusive object, constitute the truly mechanical part of reasoning; while the subject matter, presupposing always some return to the intrinsic value of the signs (and an evaluation which habits renders more or less rapid, but which can never be considered as mechanical), is the essentially reflective part.

This being granted, if when we have once connected our ideas with their signs, we could dispense with all return to the value of the latter; if, always exact and distinct from each other, they kept and represented faithfully to the eye and ear the differences as well as analogies which may exist between ideas; finally, if those ideas were all of one same kind and circumscribed in their nature, as in their signs, then the form and the subject matter of reason might be confused; the recall of the terms in a given and constant order, soon becoming a habit, might take the place of the representation of ideas, or guide it with assurance and fidelity; we could without fear let ourselves resort to the mechanism of memory which would infallibly lead to the goal; and there would thus be a general habit of reasoning, as there is one of computing, following certain methods and operations truly mechanical. But can the method be the same, when there exists an essential difference in the subjects?

The signs of quantity have, through the very nature of their subject, an undetermined representative capacity; they are signs *par excellence*. We apply numerical terms equally to everything that we can conceive of as distinct and separate; also those terms pass very promptly from the concrete to the abstract; as abstract numbers are themselves converted or transformed into the still more general signs of algebra, which shows only the relations of quantity which arithmetic must evaluate or geometry construct.

This state of indetermination and flexibility of signs permits them to be studied in themselves without actually being applied to anything that exists. All the combinations, transformations, and different modes of arrangement of which they are susceptible are read over and tables of them are drawn up. They are represented in symmetrical formulas which memory learns to retrace with promptitude. Afterwards if we pass to applications, it is no longer a question of doing anything but reattaching these familiar conventions to real objects, and since only the kind of relations expressed and predetermined in advance by the signs is examined, it will be always with these last and not really with the ideas that we will have to work. Thus, in virtue of habits acquired by the practice of the method alone, the operations of reasoning will be and remain mechanical to the end, since it will only be a question of the order of succession of the terms, of their transformations, etc., and not of their intrinsic value.

We have not and we cannot have in our usual languages flexible signs; each term represents or ought to represent a fixed and determined idea; no other term beyond can become the subject of any useful operation; it must never be isolated either in origin or in subsequent use under pain of being sundered forever.   Furthermore, since ideas are of very different kinds, all their relations cannot be evaluated or indicated in simple and invariable expressions or formulas; most of these relations are moreover of such a nature that they are not at all susceptible of being measured or exactly defined; the recall of signs cannot, therefore, take the place of or enable us to dispense absolutely with the representation of the ideas, and the form of reasoning cannot operate without subject matter.

When we reason with words, we have, therefore, always the two sorts of preceding operations to execute.   The one consists in recalling the signs in a certain order (given by the construction of the language of which we have made a habit); this operation is mechanical and can be likened to the processes of computation; the order of construction may favor the representation of ideas, as we have seen (Chapter IV), but it no longer actually occupies us.   It leads us, we do not lead it, and leaves all the powers of our thought in reserve for the second operation.   This consists in appreciating (in proportion as we progress) the value of the terms and in returning to the ideas which they express; a return more or less easy, rapid, and flexible, according as the ideas are more or less familiar, but which can never be wholly replaced by mechanical habits without the dangers which we have previously recognized.

In short, in calculation and particularly in the processes of algebraical analysis, we need only think in the beginning of the operation, in arranging or translating the data of the problem; the method afterwards executes all the rest without our

having any need of thinking of it; it alone works the transformations, the solution of the unknown quantities, etc.

In our reasonings with words, we can profitably advance
only by the help of representative memory. It is not enough
that it furnishes the terms in the order predetermined by habit;
if questioned as to their title, it is forced each time to give an
account of it. The more judgments or different propositions
there are in the same reasoning, the more problems there are
to equate and solve; attention depends only an instant upon
the efficiency of the habitual method in order to arise the
instant after.

Let us conclude: since our reasonings are not only in the
form, therefore they cannot be conducted by absolutely mechanical operations. There is, therefore, no general habit which
directs us or which can direct us in the art of reasoning, as
there is in the art of computing.

If the project of a universal language, closely imitating algebra, or of a kind of written symbolism of general applicability
(spécieuse générale) (such as Leibnitz[1] and other learned men
have conceived) could ever be effected, the operations of reasoning would then become purely mechanical like those of calculation. Then, reduced to taking all the proportions and measur-
ing all the relations of the signs alone (and no longer the
relations of the ideas themselves, as in the actual state of
things), we would have a general method, which, converted into
a habit, would guide the solution of every kind of problems,
without our needing to think of it, with that assurance and
rapidity which habit gives to the processes of algebraical analysis. But I believe that it is demonstrated today (and all that
has been said finally, in the course of this memoir, on the different functions of our signs, tends to confirm it) that such a
language could neither be reconciled with the nature of our
mixed ideas nor with the needs of our diverse faculties, which
always brings us back to the same conclusion.

[1] See the *Lettres de Leibnitz et l'eloge de ce grand homme* by Bailly. *Spécieuse mathématique* means algebra.—TR.

We are perhaps, as to the practice of our languages—both common and scientific—in a position comparable to that of the ancient geometers, who, without knowing our algebra, did with it nevertheless some very great things by uniting geometrical synthesis and analysis. They operated with figures and we operate with ideas; their reasonings gradually advanced by developing and compounding; their memory had to carry at the same time the double load of signs and ideas. They were ignorant of the use of those instruments, of those levers which centuple the powers of thought by saving them labor; they had not discovered the art of comprehending in abridged formulas the results of the longest deductions, of expressing the ratios composed of the parts of space by very simple ratios, which rest the senses and give wings to memory; but precisely because they lacked levers, their heads became more powerful. Also the productions of the ancients bear the impress of an energy and vigor which astonishes us and surpasses us; and while children solve with a dash of the pen problems which those geniuses—limited to their own powers—could not attain or attained only with the greatest efforts, the teachers in their turn sometimes have much difficulty in following to the end the synthetic chain of their ideas. So it is by walking first in the footprints of the inventors, by being trained in the same manner that most of our great geometers are formed; it is this old method that they recommend, as if through gratitude; finally it is this alone which the great Newton found worthy of interpreting his genius! If the universal language could some day change reasoning to calculation, substitute an easy and certain mechanism for the slow and often uncertain representation of ideas, without doubt the art of reasoning would experience a revolution as fortunate as that which the exact sciences owe to the application of algebra to geometry. But the more the progress of human knowledge would suddenly extend, the more would the genius acquire power by joining his own power to that of a new instrument; the more perhaps would perfectibility be restrained in consequence; the more would the faculties common to men lose their activity, by the extreme facility of their action. This would be the triumph of habit! Then, doubtless, there would arise philosophers who would seek to check this mechanism, would come back to the old method, would recommend its practice, would translate their results into it after having obtained them too easily in the new way (*ut lumen publicum sustinere valerent*, as Newton himself said, in speaking of the synthetic translation).

Then those who have exclusively practiced the generally applicable symbolism and who had made a habit of it, would solve without difficulty many problems of psychology and ideology, around which we turn so laboriously and would perhaps believe themselves superior men, whereas they could not bear, without being overcome, the reading of the profound thinkers of our day. Mental levers are like physical levers; they aid us, but sometimes too much, by hindering the development of our natural powers. Also, when they abandon us, we are delivered helpless to every weakness which proceeds from their habitual use. All this brings us back to the method and means indicated (in Chapter IV of this section) for the object of developing good memory habits, and of forming and keeping that just temper, that equilibrium of the powers of thought. To exercise by appropriate means all the powers, but gradually and without ever overworking them; to make a habit, a necessity of representing ideas clearly and of connecting them with their signs; to keep ourselves from being led by words and purely mechanical forms; such are the first conditions which a method must fulfil in order to attain the end proposed. But one cannot deny that synthesis is that which contributes to it first most directly. This is not that obscure method, justly proscribed by Condillac, which is composed only of chimeras, which starts from vague abstract principles as their source of evidence, piles them one upon another and incessantly and laboriously revolves in the hollow sphere of verbal identities; but that synthesis which our common master has himself often practiced under another name; the one which conforms to the direct order of the formation of ideas, acknowledges at first only the simplest elements, that is to say, those clearest and best determined (see Chapter IV), successively combines them with each other, makes signs only in making ideas, and always imposes upon itself the necessary law of retracing them conjointly. This method, with which thought always knows whence it comes and where it is, advances slowly, but with certainty, without ever forgetting or losing sight of itself; can stop at will or continue its progress; passes from darkness to light through well controlled gradations, is led in short without being hurried along, enlightened without being dazzled.

It is the practice of such a method which conserves to thought its fortunate independence, provides beforehand against the dangerous precipice of mechanical habits, inspires it with that suspicion which permits no doubtful terms or elements, often brings them back for examination, remakes them or verifies them: salutary distrust, the example and the precept of which true philosophers give us, the only counterbalance of blind habit, the source of wisdom and the active cause of all real progress!

CONCLUSION

Ideology can rise above general grammar and penetrate the external forms of thought or the signs with which it is clothed to those internal and profound modifications the signs of which are drawn only from the knowledge of the laws of our organisation, from the study or feeling of that close connection which exists between the physical and the mental in our being. This connection, in fact, may be felt and observed; it is felt by those individuals whom a delicate temperament and a sort of uneasiness in the vital functions incessantly turn back upon themselves, who hear, so to say, the springs of the machine creaking and feel that thought strains or relaxes with them. It is observed and demonstrated with proof by those philosophers who have apprehended and compared sensible nature in its different states, followed the course of affections and ideas in the organic variations corresponding to ages, powers, temperaments, etc.; they alone "have *seen phenomena,* the machine alternately calm or disturbed, weak or vigorous, healthy or broken, destructive or under control; successively imbecile, enlightened, stupid, blustering, mute, lethargic, active, living, dead."[2]

In order to treat thoroughly the question proposed, it would have been necessary first to be in possession in its entirety of that general grammar or science of our ideas and of our signs considered in their reciprocal relations; for the external forms of thought are thrown into the mould of languages; the terms of which these languages are composed are repeated at each moment and our most numerous and striking habits are connected with their use.

But it would particularly have been necessary to join to the *feeling* of those inner modifications, of those profound habits of thought, the knowledge of the signs proper to express them; it would have been necessary to have in our possession the terms for necessary relations in order to compare the influence of habit in the physical and the mental realms, in the operations of life and in those of intelligence, in the functions of motor and sensory organs and in those upon which the different modes of thought depend. The question itself invoked those comparisons. It furnished the finest opportunity to *carry physiology into ideology,* or to tighten even more closely the bonds which must henceforth unite those two sciences. I have dared to look upon this distant goal. I have tried to approach it. I have borrowed from sources which might furnish me with the means to this end. It is to more enlightened men, to better heads than mine that it belongs to accomplish what I have anticipated.

1. Physiologists distinguish living forces into *sensory* and *motor.* While meditating upon the data of my subject, I have recognized, or thought I recognized, that it was necessary to introduce the same distinction into the analysis of impressions and ideas.

---

[2] See the article on Locke, *Encyclopédie ancienne.*

What external signs and experiments, made directly upon sensitive and irritable parts, make clear to the physician is revealed in another way to the consciousness of the reflective observer, who compares himself introspectively in the exercise of the functions of his senses. He feels himself passive in certain impressions, active in others. He recognizes that there is in him one force which *feels* and another which *moves* (feeling and will), that these two forces combined take turns in predominating over each other and concur, in a very unequal manner, in the different impressions which he receives.

In examining the external senses first, some seem to be endowed with a particular mobility, while others are or appear quite immobile; the latter have a more exquisite feeling, their impressions are all excitative; the former are more delicate than sensitive and their very sensibility seems to be subordinate to the movement which directs and tempers it. The individual *perceives* through these latter organs; he is affected, he *feels* (in the whole meaning of the word) through the former; *sensation* differs from *perception*.

The being reduced to passive immobile organs, or organs by which he would not perceive, would not initiate movements, would be limited to instinctive faculties; there would not be a distinct personality in him. By smell alone, for example, his existence would perhaps be comparable to that of the oyster or the polyp; so far would he be from being capable of forming combinations, abstractions, etc. Every active and perfectible faculty begins with perception and voluntary movement. (We have explained the word *voluntary*.)

The action of thought in the absence of objects is only the repetition of that action which has been exerted by the senses upon those objects. The central organ can retain the determination caused by sense and likewise bring it about by an action which is peculiar to it. But it directly acts to elaborate, combine and reproduce only the impressions transmitted by mobile organs or submitted to voluntary action. There are, therefore, no *ideas* corresponding to *pure sensations*, but only to *perceptions*. The ideas are images or copies: some are reproduced spontaneously, others are recalled by a renewed act of the will which coöperated to form them. There is no recall without the movements and impressions which are associated with them. These movements are the signs of the impressions. The signs are *natural* or *artificial* according as the association is formed in the very act of the perception by the coöperation of motor and sensory organs or by a deliberate and subsequent determination of will.

The faculty of recalling constitutes what we generally call *memory*. Its action is based essentially on movements or associated signs.

The imagination consists in the spontaneous reproduction of images. Objects themselves, associated in a common perception, fulfill for it the function of signs. It is also put into activity by the internal organs and often receives laws from them. Imagination differs from memory as sensation differs from perception.

2. Sensation, continued or repeated, fades, is gradually obscured and ends by disappearing without leaving any trace. Repeated movement gradually becomes more precise, more prompt, and easier. Increasing facility corresponds to the weakening of the *effort;* and if this effort should become nil, there would be no more consciousness of movement, no more volition; but, whatever degree of facility the movement attains, there almost always remains a memory, a determination made by the original effort; and even when the motor activity has become almost insensible to the individual who executes it, its product is only more assured and distinct.

If all our faculties and operations by whatever name they are distinguished, are only modifications of those of feeling or movement, they must participate in one or the other of those two influences of habit; to become distorted, to deteriorate (and in certain cases to become heightened) as sensations or feelings, to be developed or perfected, to acquire more precision, rapidity, facility in their exercise, as movements. The influence of habit is a sure test, to which we can submit our faculties in order to recognize the identity or diversity of their origin; all those which will be modified in the same way by passing through this test, must be grouped in the same class, and those which will not will be in different classes. While sensation repeated becomes weaker in the organ or any non-central part whatsoever directly excited, the sensitive principle or the system may keep its determination, tend to bring it about in the accustomed intervals, claim the same springs of irritation, get exasperated at their absence. Hence comes *desire*, produced by the instinct of the organs, which gives laws to the will without receiving any from it and can take place without will, movement or power. This is why sensations, while weakening through habit, are nevertheless transformed into imperious needs.

If any exciting cause whatsoever were directly applied to a center or seat of sensibility, the affections, far from becoming weakened, would only increase in energy. Thus all the passions—natural or artificial—all the feelings, first awakened by images or produced and afterwards determined by the dispositions of the internal organs, these images themselves, when they arise from the continued heightening of cerebral sensitivity, etc., only succeed in being strengthened by the duration or the repetition of the causes which produce them.

Organs of sensation or desire are blunted rather than perfected by repeated exercise. If their impressions (in certain cases) seem always to keep or recover the same freshness, it is because they are revived by tendencies periodically arising from centers which correspond to them; aside from that, their characteristic sensitivity effervesces in its exercise and their movements, which are executed from the first with confidence, hardly improve by being repeated.

Habit first influences the organs of perception by moderating their sensitivity, which was too delicate in the beginning. This very effect prepares and contributes to favor the development of their characteristic mobility. Hence begins true progress in the operations and faculties directly allied to the exercise of the senses. But the easier the movements become, the more the perception, which depends upon them, acquires precision and clearness, the more also the individual misunderstands the part that he plays in them, the more his activity is disguised. The object and the end of the action, effort and resistance are finally almost identified, everything seems to wear the passive character of sensation.

A host of operations and judgments crowd round this perception, which has become so rapid and apparently so simple. Here one must necessarily go back from the partial activity of the external senses to that of the central organ, which reunites and combines their impressions, transforms and changes them into each other.

From two or more different perceptions, which are separate in their organs, but constantly repeated together, results almost always a single mixed impression, which must be considered a real resultant of all those that compose it, since it proceeds from all simultaneously, without being any one of them in particular. Hence it happens in the first place, that an impression which, if it were isolated, would approach the passive character, acquires the activity which it lacks by its combination with another in which mobility predominates. This effect is manifest in the intimate association of sight with touch, and especially of hearing with the vocal organ. A man who understands without the faculty of speech, would hardly distinguish sounds, and certainly he would not recall them.

It happens in the second place that impressions, thus associated and transformed in a common center, no longer receive their type of action itself from the senses which they directly concern, but from the inner fire of the central organ, which, reacting with the sum of its acquired determinations, changes, complicates, corrects, and sometimes misrepresents the simple reports of the external senses, substitutes memories for perception, and objectifies what has existed rather than perceives what exists. Hence the confirmation of that sentence of a great philosopher: *"Omnes perceptiones tam sensus, quam mentis, sunt ex analogia hominis, non ex analogia universi,"* etc. Hence the rapidity and certainty with which we perceive or think we perceive actually by one sense what is not at all in its domain, or what obviously exceeds its reach. Hence a multitude of illusions so much the more difficult to destroy the older they are and the more the most authentic testimony and the most frequent experiences seem constantly to substantiate them. Hence the order established by the habits of the imagination is confused with the nature of the things; there is a presupposition of a fixed and necessary existence where there exists only a fortuitous and transitory coincidence; the generalization of particular experiences, the conversion of the relative into the absolute, of false reports of essentiality into habitually simultaneous impressions, those of causality into the familiar order of the successive.

Hence the certainty with which we await phenomena which always have followed each other uniformly; the want of foresight of contrary chances, the trouble, the surprise, the wonder or the fear which they inspire when realized, the emotion in time of change, the indifference in time of uniformity; hence in short that multitude of judgments which are blended for us in sensation itself and always (for the same reason) because the numerous movements, as much internal as external on which they depend, have become extremely rapid and easy; and because the attention no longer excited by effort or the movement itself which it directed in the beginning, remains inactive and abandons all to the force of habit and imagination.

Habit influences our perceptive faculty, as well as simple motor activities. This faculty takes its rise in movement. If, as Bonnet has said, *perception differs from sensation only in degree,* it must also tend to be gradually obscured and heightened and would not be susceptible of any progress.

3. All operations whatsoever, when they are frequently repeated, cease providing the central motor organ with that activity which, giving it consciousness of its powers, in some fashion constituted its life.

The first movements associated with impressions, being continually repeated from the beginning, become insensible in consequence of the very perfecting of the organs. Their natural functions as signs are absolutely forgotten or miscomprehended. There is no more free recall. All is under the power of the imagination.

The secondary signs of language fortunately come to moderate this mobility of habit, to reveal to the individual the kind of sway that he could exercise upon many of those modifications, to create for him a second memory.

Among the voluntary movements which can serve equally well as signs of recall, those of the voice, beside the freedom and the perfect ease of their exercise, have the unique and infinitely precious advantage of making the individual doubly present to himself, by the effort which they determine and by the impression which they produce; they justify the preference which is accorded to them in mental or social communications.

The individual notes by articulated signs all that he feels, perceives, or imagines in himself or outside himself. But the nature of the impressions with which he associates his vocal movements, the manner in which he forms these first associations, that in which habit later succeeds in modifying them, limits the general utility which was promised or corrupts its first fruits.

Articulated sound is a perception; it can contract the fixed and narrow bond only with impressions of a nature homogeneous with its own.

Sensations, obscure or fleeting modifications, variable feelings, phantoms, really archetypal ideas, all those vain and illusory products of an excited brain, receive no light, no real fixity (but too often a deceptive consistancy) from vocal notes intended to express or recall them.

In the second place, although named perceptions are circumscribed and persistant in themselves, it often happens that attention or motor activity does not develop them in a common act, is not divided equally between signs and things. Then association is irregular or non-existent; the sign alone remains empty in memory or the idea is isolated in the imagination and afterwards escapes active recall.

Finally, extreme facility in articulation or the mechanical recall of signs, coming from very frequent repetition, may end by disordering their most useful functions (in the same way that it had already annulled the functions of the first signs) and deliver once again the imagination without check over to its own sallies.

From whatever cause the isolation of the sign proceeds, every time its recall is void of representation, memory is *mechanical*.

If, by the nature of associated modifications, the sign has only an excitative power in some degree without any determined or determinable value, memory is *sensory*.

In the sole cases where association, which is regularly formed with distinct perceptions, gives the signs the infallible power of evoking ideas or images, memory is *representative*.

Habit influences mechanical memory as well as the faculty of merely moving; sensory memory, as well as that of feeling; representative memory, as well as that of perceiving.

In the first case, there is a series of prompt, easy, unperceived and finally almost automatic movements; in the second, a series of modifications, emotions, phantoms evoked by articulated sounds, now a weakening, now a heightening in the sensory effect, perpetual vicissitudes in the thing signified, permanence of the sign, illusory judgment which transfers to the one all the fixity of the other.

In the third case, there is a series of signs and ideas, woven together in the same chain; prompter, surer, easier (and perhaps too easy) recall of some, but always fidelity, clearness of representation of others. This is the only useful memory and the sole basis of human intelligence.

In mechanical memory, movement absorbs all the powers of the thinking organ; the sensory memory makes sensitivity predominate over the motor powers; the latter forms and sustains that just equilibrium on which reason depends in mental affairs as health in physical.

Frequent repetition of the same articulated signs modifies in a very remarkable way the judgments which we make about facts, as well as the relations of our ideas among themselves or of terms among themselves or of the one with the other.

A primary habit hardly permits us to conceive of an object, of any *idea* whatsoever, without recalling the *sign* which expresses it (although the effect is very far from being reciprocal). By dint of thus perceiving and contemplating both, we soon end by not being able to isolate them absolutely. They seem to us to participate in the same essence. It is especially in the use of archetypal terms that this judgment is involved by an invincible power; the sign then appears to take in memory the place of external resistance. These are two bonds which equally unite impressions associated by simultaneity, two habits almost as old, almost as profound. Hence the magic power of the terms *substance, essence,* etc.; the reifying of abstract or general nouns; the long-standing errors of the scholastics and metaphysicians (up to Locke); hence the extreme difficulty which in consequence there must be in separating signs and ideas. Honor to the philosopher who first completed this separation and succeeded in dissolving that aggregate, cemented by the habits of centuries! He was truly the creator of logic and ideology.

All the habitual forms of our language lead us to reify abstractions and although in theory we know very well what to think, the best minds may be deceived in practice by this illusion of habit, as they are in relating colors to objects.

Woe to reason, when language has perpetuated meaningless expressions, false or foolish judgments! Their continual repetition transforms them into habits of the ear or voice and afterwards the terms acquire a title to belief which, removing from them all suspicion, causes them to be passed blindly along without the least investigation. Such is the power of habits of speech, that there is perhaps no absurdity of which we do not end by being convinced by repeating often and for a long time the signs which express it! . . . .

Our judgments are mechanical, when they are founded only upon the repetition of the same senseless terms. The memory of having always believed or articulated the same words, takes the place of any other proof and this routine confidence, this mechanical faith increases precisely as the number of repetitions augments. Its obstinacy is proportional to its blindness: both prove the power of habit.

The best founded rights as well as the most chimerical, the most real as well as the most false, in short *reflective* judgments as well as mechanical judgments acquire new weight by the sole fact of their repetition. But all that happens exclusively under the sway of habit should lose its authority before the eyes of reason.

Habit furthermore substitutes simple memories for the direct perception of evidence, which is the first ground of reflective judgment. It transfers to some the legitimate confidence which others enjoy, hides their real motives from us and is opposed with increasing force to new verifications, replaces the doubt of wisdom by a blind presumption, the need of knowing by apathetic indifference to known verities. This is why it often hides our first errors and perpetuates them, covers with mists the source of truths and circumscribes their influence.

As soon as we no longer pass judgment except on *memories*, the longest reasonings should acquire a rapidity equal to that of the simple succession of the terms of which they are composed. But the habits of memory tend to increase this rapidity indefinitely. Then reflection is banished, attention is no more, and all is again given over to pure mechanism.

The most complicated operations are, it is true, executed with assurance and facility, but thought sleeps and loses its powers in inaction. Philosophical analysis can arise in the midst of this general temptation, as the most powerful resources of industry in great necessities. But it seeks elements and finds only firmly aggregated masses; it seeks a foundation where it can be attached and finds only airy forms which escape it; it wishes to direct and point the good road and all flee before it down the most rapid descent; then, changing its name as well as its functions, this analysis will no longer be that which severs, but that which unites.

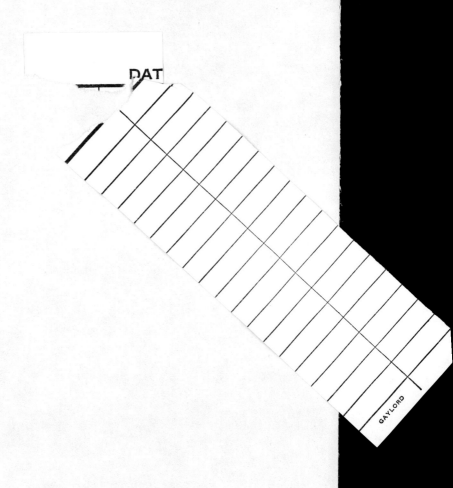

DAT